PRACTICAL SOLUTIONS FOR POTTERS

Practical Solutions for Potters

100s of your top questions with 1000s of practical solutions

Gill Bliss

Sterling Publishing Co., Inc.
New York
A Sterling/Silver Book

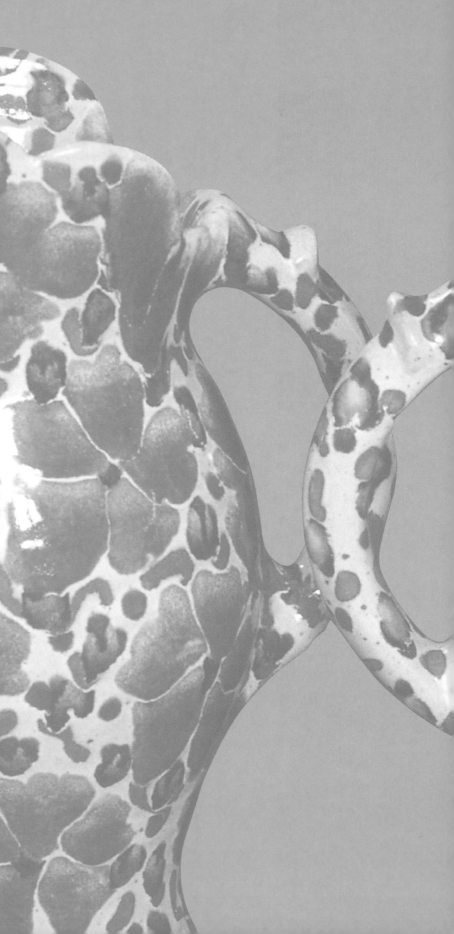

A QUARTO BOOK

Library of Congress Cataloging-in-Publication
Data is available upon request

Published by Sterling Publishing Co., Inc
387 Park Avenue South
New York, N.Y. 10016-8810

Distributed in Canada by Sterling Publishing
c/o Canadian Manda Group,
One Atlantic Avenue, Suite 105
Toronto, Ontario, Canada M6K 3EF

This book was designed and produced by
Quarto Publishing plc, The Old Brewery
6 Blundell Street, London N7 6BH

Senior editor **Michelle Pickering**
Editor **Mary Senechal**
Senior art editor **Elizabeth Healey**
Designer **Ellen Moorcraft**
Illustrators **Kevin Maddison**
Photographer **Patricia Aithie/ffotograff**
Art director **Moira Clinch**
Assistant art director **Penny Cobb**

Typeset by Central Southern Typesetters,
Eastbourne, UK
Manufactured by Eray Scan Pte Ltd, Singapore
Printed by Leefung-Asco Printers Ltd, China

ISBN 0-8069-6307-7 (hardcover)
ISBN 0-8069-6741-2 (paperback)

NOTE
Using pottery-making materials and equipment
can be dangerous if safety precautions are not
adhered to. Always exercise caution, and seek
the advice of the manufacturers if in doubt.
Suggested safety precautions are stated
throughout the book where relevant; a
summary can also be found on page 188.

*The ceramics pictured on these and the previous
two pages are by **Clive Davies***

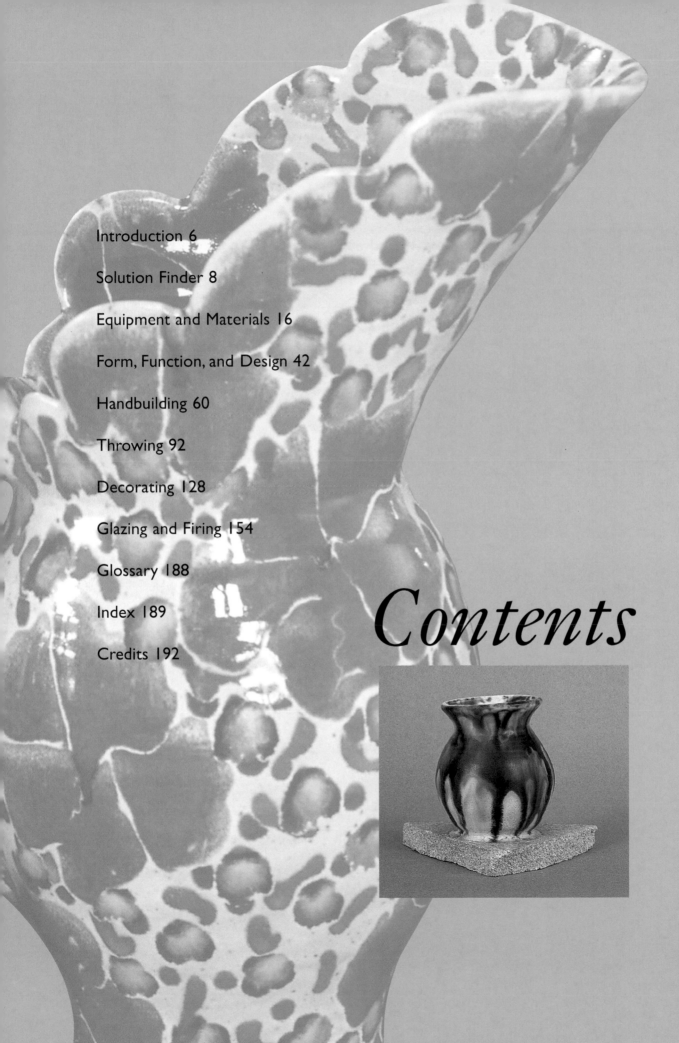

Contents

Introduction

Clay is an exciting material, which can be used to create an infinite variety of objects, from everyday functional items to huge public sculptures. Techniques for shaping, decorating, and finishing ceramics have been passed down through history, and knowledge from past generations is continually being added to with fresh insights and technical developments.

Left: Clive Davies, Pitchers
Far right: Janet Hamer,
A gaggle of geese

The best way to learn about making pottery is, of course, by experimenting for yourself. There is no substitute for hands-on practice: manipulating coils of clay, throwing on a wheel, painting with ceramic colors, experimenting with and testing glaze mixes. Working through difficulties and finding solutions to problems is part and parcel of finding your own individual way of using clay. Practical experience will build your confidence and hone your skills.

Sometimes, however, a helpful hint or timely explanation from a friendly potter or teacher can save hours of struggle and frustration, and it is with this in mind that this book has been written. It seeks to solve the problems that can arise in a clear and direct manner, in a simple question-and-answer format.

Many of the questions have several answers. Very often when using clay there is no one right way of proceeding, no definitive answer or single route to follow. What I have sought to do in this book, therefore, is to provide sufficient guidance to help you find the solutions that are most appropriate for your style of work.

Solution
Finder

THERE ARE THREE WAYS TO ACCESS THE ANSWER TO YOUR PARTICULAR PROBLEM. Firstly, you can read through the chapter that relates to your area of interest from beginning to end. Secondly, you can access a specific topic by using the index on pages 189–191. The third method is to use this solution finder. Each chapter of the book is examined in turn and broken down into categories; the numbers listed after each category refer to those pages on which you will find questions and answers on that particular subject.

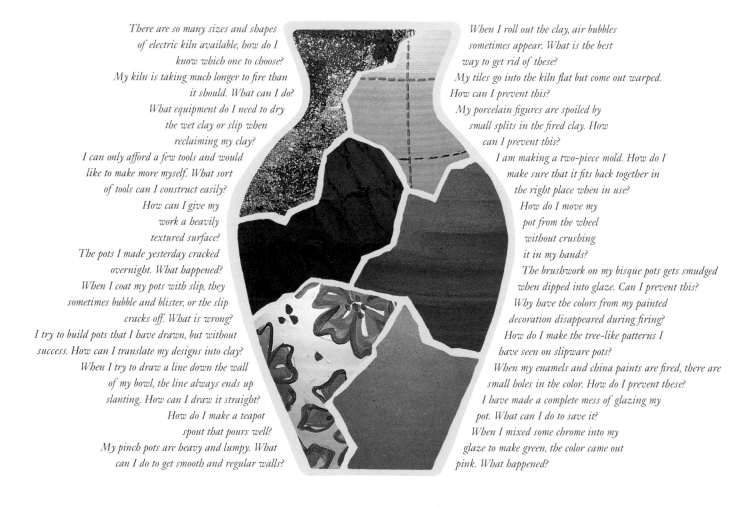

There are so many sizes and shapes of electric kiln available, how do I know which one to choose?

My kiln is taking much longer to fire than it should. What can I do?

What equipment do I need to dry the wet clay or slip when reclaiming my clay?

I can only afford a few tools and would like to make more myself. What sort of tools can I construct easily?

How can I give my work a heavily textured surface?

The pots I made yesterday cracked overnight. What happened?

When I coat my pots with slip, they sometimes bubble and blister, or the slip cracks off. What is wrong?

I try to build pots that I have drawn, but without success. How can I translate my designs into clay?

When I try to draw a line down the wall of my bowl, the line always ends up slanting. How can I draw it straight?

How do I make a teapot spout that pours well?

My pinch pots are heavy and lumpy. What can I do to get smooth and regular walls?

When I roll out the clay, air bubbles sometimes appear. What is the best way to get rid of these?

My tiles go into the kiln flat but come out warped. How can I prevent this?

My porcelain figures are spoiled by small splits in the fired clay. How can I prevent this?

I am making a two-piece mold. How do I make sure that it fits back together in the right place when in use?

How do I move my pot from the wheel without crushing it in my hands?

The brushwork on my bisque pots gets smudged when dipped into glaze. Can I prevent this?

Why have the colors from my painted decoration disappeared during firing?

How do I make the tree-like patterns I have seen on slipware pots?

When my enamels and china paints are fired, there are small holes in the color. How do I prevent these?

I have made a complete mess of glazing my pot. What can I do to save it?

When I mixed some chrome into my glaze to make green, the color came out pink. What happened?

What is the best equipment to buy and how do I maintain it?

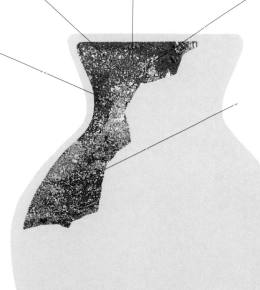

I want to invest in some tools. What should I buy?

Equipment and Materials pages 16–41

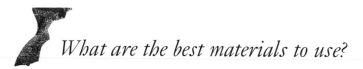

What are the best materials to use?

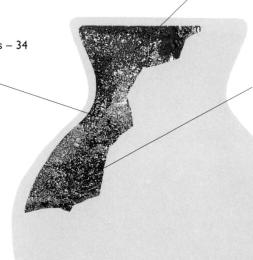

Equipment
and *Materials* pages 16–41

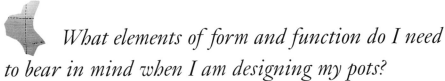

*What elements of form and function do I need
to bear in mind when I am designing my pots?*

Form, Function, and Design pages 42–59

*My handbuilt pots and figurative sculptures
do not turn out the way I want. Can you help?*

Handbuilding pages 60–91

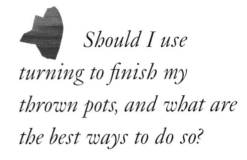

 I am unhappy with my thrown pots. How can I achieve more successful results?

Should I use turning to finish my thrown pots, and what are the best ways to do so?

Throwing pages 92–127

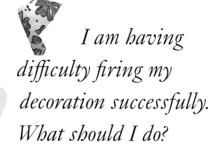

What kinds of decoration can I use to make my pottery more exciting?

I am having difficulty firing my decoration successfully. What should I do?

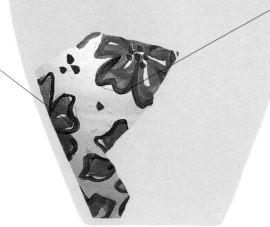

Decorating pages 128–153

How do I glaze my pots?

Glazing – the basics
* Types of glaze – 155, 166, 167, 170, 172, 173
* Glaze ingredients – 156, 166, 167, 168, 169, 170, 172, 173
* Equipment – 156, 157, 158, 163, 164
* Mixing glazes – 156, 157, 158
* Testing glazes – 157, 159, 163
* Applying glazes – 157, 160, 161, 162, 163, 164, 165, 166, 170, 173
* Colored glazes – 167, 168, 169, 173, 174
* Firing glazes – 155, 165, 166, 167, 169, 170, 172, 173, 181

Special glaze effects
* Crazing – 171
* Crawling – 171
* Crater glazes – 172
* Crystalline glazes – 172, 173
* Reduction glazes – 173, 174, 182
* Salt glazes – 174
* Raku glazes – 174

What is the best way to fire my pots?

Firing – the basics
* Packing your kiln – 175, 176
* Kiln shelves and furniture – 175, 176
* Firing cycles – 175, 177, 178, 180, 182, 183
* Cones – 177, 178, 179, 187
* Bungs – 179
* See also: kiln equipment, pages 17–23

Troubleshooting
* Problems with kilns – 177, 178, 180
* Pots damaged during firing – 175, 180, 181, 183, 186

Decorative firing techniques
* Smoke firing – 183, 184, 185
* Raku firing – 186, 187
* Salt firing – 187

Glazing and Firing pages 154–187

IT IS POSSIBLE to make pottery by digging clay from the ground and firing pots in a bonfire, but most of us wish to make use of the wonderful modern advances in clays, glazes, and kiln design. Selecting the right tools and equipment, and keeping them in good order, are important aspects of being a potter, and understanding how to use the wealth of materials available adds to the excitement of creating in clay.

Equipment and *Materials*

I would like to fire my pottery at home, but I do not have much space. Is there a kiln that is easy to install?

Small kilns

You can buy a small electric kiln of about 1 cubic foot (200cc) capacity, which plugs into a regular electric socket. These kilns are a useful solution in situations where the size and wiring makes the installation of a larger model impractical. Even a small kiln must have adequate ventilation and space when firing, but you can push it into a corner when it is not in use.

I want to use my garage as a pottery studio, but do not want the cost of putting in special wiring for the kiln. What do you suggest?

In a workshop that does not have an adequate electric power supply, a kiln run from bottled gas can be the answer. Check with the kiln supplier for any legal or safety restrictions on the siting of the kiln you choose to buy. Gas kilns are usually more expensive to buy than electric ones, but you do not have the cost of replacing elements. With gas, you also have the advantage of being able to choose a reducing atmosphere. However, you must site a gas kiln more carefully than an electric kiln because of the emissions produced.

Can I harden a few pots without a kiln – using my oven, for example?

Firing without a kiln

The temperature at which clay changes its chemical composition and becomes a hard, ceramic material is 1110°F (600°C). A domestic oven cannot reach this temperature and is therefore not a possible substitute for a kiln.

There are many places in the world, however, such as parts of Africa and India, where pots are fired without the use of modern kiln technology. You can fire your pots in a similar way, simply by building a bonfire around them. You will need to keep stoking your bonfire in order to reach a hot enough temperature, and you are liable to lose quite a few pots because of thermal shock.

More elaborate versions of a bonfire firing include digging a pit in the ground, or using a container such as a metal garbage can or a brick construction to contain the burning material.

Bonfire firing

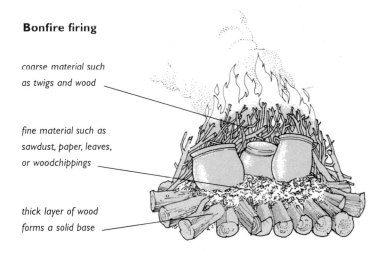

coarse material such as twigs and wood

fine material such as sawdust, paper, leaves, or woodchippings

thick layer of wood forms a solid base

Container firing

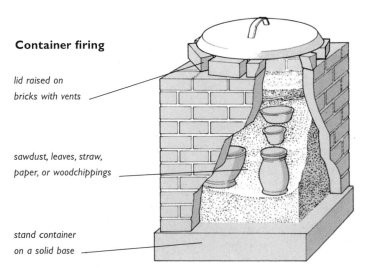

lid raised on bricks with vents

sawdust, leaves, straw, paper, or woodchippings

stand container on a solid base

There are so many sizes and shapes of electric kiln available, how do I know which one to choose?

Look first at the restrictions imposed by your particular circumstances. How much electricity can you use? Will you be using your normal household supply or a separate supply for your kiln? How big a space do you have for the kiln, and what size are the entrances through which you must bring it? Second, think about the kind of work you want to make. Do you need a kiln chamber that is tall or wide? Will you be firing large kiln-loads of thrown ware or a small quantity of decorative pieces? This will help you to decide the size and shape of kiln you need. Lastly, the cost of a new kiln or the availability of a secondhand one may be the determining factor.

I have a secondhand pottery kiln which does not have any kiln furniture. Can I make my own?

Furniture fit for firing

Kiln furniture is made from best-quality refractory clays that can withstand the high temperature of firings. It is inadvisable to use homemade pottery substitutes, which may split and warp. Clays used for making pottery are pyroplastic, which means they become soft during firing and harden again when fully fired. Kiln furniture made in ordinary clay would, therefore, slump very readily.

What are the differences between a top-loading and front-loading kiln?

Front-loading kilns

Front-loading kilns have a more solid metal framework and thicker walls than top loaders, which means they retain heat for longer. They are also more expensive to buy and install, but are harder wearing and will have a longer life. They are heavy, so you will need to think carefully about how to maneuver the kiln into position.

Top-loading kilns

Top-loading kilns are convenient for small-scale workshops, as they are cheaper to buy and easier to install. Some potters feel that top loaders cool too rapidly, having a detrimental effect on their work. Others consider this an advantage, as they are able to have a very quick firing cycle. This is really a matter of personal preference.

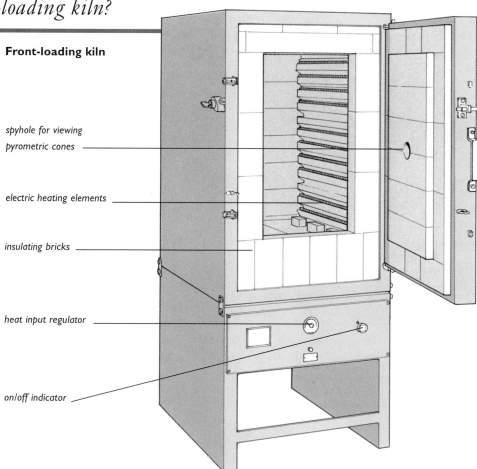

Front-loading kiln

spyhole for viewing pyrometric cones

electric heating elements

insulating bricks

heat input regulator

on/off indicator

I need to build up some shelves to pack my kiln. Where do I put the props?

Line up your props

All props should be aligned underneath each other from one shelf to the next, so that the weight is taken down through the props. A shelf without proper support can warp or split, particularly during high-temperature firings. Keep the line of props out of the way of any bunghole that may be used to view cones.

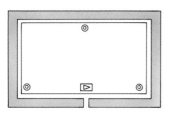

BUILD IN THREES

Whether you have circular or rectangular shelves, position three props for each shelf. Rectangular shelves that have been supported at four corners will quickly sag in the middle, whereas the triangular tensions running across shelves supported by three props will help to keep the shelf flat.

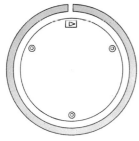

◎ *position of props*

▷ *position of cones in front of spyhole*

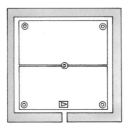

SPLIT SHELVES

If you have two rectangular shelves for each layer, it is possible to position a central prop that supports both shelves but which will not block a spyhole at the front of the kiln.

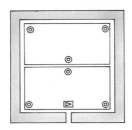

◎ *position of props*

▷ *position of cones in front of spyhole*

When I unpack my kiln, the props stick to the shelves. How can I prevent this?

When unpacking your kiln, give each shelf a wiggle before lifting. This should release any props that are slightly stuck to the shelves, and prevent work being damaged by falling props.

How can I prevent my kiln shelves from warping?

To prevent warping, check that your shelves are thick enough for the weight and temperature of your firings, and turn your shelves for each firing so that both sides are used alternately. If your shelves have already warped, turn them over so that they gradually warp back in future firings until flat.

How can I be sure that I will not leave my kiln firing for too long?

Your kiln should be fitted with a controller that switches it off automatically when a given temperature is reached. Some can also be programmed to turn the kiln off after a set number of hours, so that it does not continue to fire if the correct temperature cannot be reached due to a burned-out element. Even with these precautions, leaving a firing kiln to its own devices for a weekend, or while you take a vacation, is asking for trouble. It is better to get into the habit of checking your kiln several times during firing, and watching for the time when the top temperature is reached.

There are many different kiln controllers available. What facilities do they offer?

The simplest controllers switch the kiln off at a chosen temperature, which is measured either by a thermocouple inside the kiln or by the bending of a cone placed in a special kiln sitter. Many can also hold the kiln at a pre-set temperature to maintain "soaking." The most advanced equipment consists of computers that can control all aspects of firing: when the kiln switches on and off; the rate of the temperature rise; whether there is a soak at any point; and for how long, and how quickly, the kiln cools. There are also controllers that offer a happy medium between these two types, so that you can choose the aspects you prefer to be automatic and those you want to operate manually.

Is there any way to judge the temperature of the kiln without a built-in controller?

Melting cones
You can place numbered temperature cones inside the kiln. The cones are manufactured from glaze materials that melt at designated temperatures, indicated by the number of cone you choose. The melting cones viewed through a bunghole tell you when a particular temperature has been reached.

Using a pyrometer
A pyrometer measures temperatures beyond the range of ordinary thermometers. It works with a thermocouple, which is a probe that you put into the kiln. Although they are usually built into a kiln, you can buy an independent thermocouple and pyrometer. Thermocouples are very fragile, and those which have a metal casing are more suited for this type of use.

My kiln always seems to be littered with crumbs and dust. How can I keep it clean?

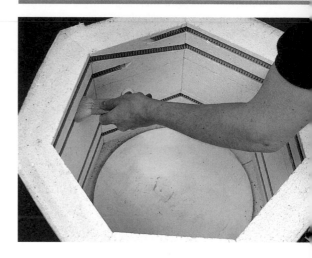

Brushing
Unwanted debris must be cleared, because it can contaminate elements, shelves, and your work. Use a soft paintbrush to dust around the elements, and a dustpan and brush to clean the floor of the kiln.

Vacuuming
A small vacuum cleaner is very useful for sucking up debris from the corners and floor of the kiln. It will pull unwanted particles from around the elements, which are difficult to reach with a brush.

The elements in my kiln need replacing several times a year. Can I do anything to make them last longer?

Lower your firing temperature
Elements continually fired to stoneware temperatures, which are usually in the region of 2190°–2370°F (1200°–1300°C), have a shorter life than those used for earthenware firings. Firing to 2300°F (1260°C) and above causes particular wear on the elements, so many stoneware potters now choose a slightly lower temperature of 2265°F (1240°C) or 2230°F (1220°C).

Remove debris
Keep your kiln free from debris. Droplets of glaze are especially harmful, because they can burn through an affected element and drastically reduce its life.

Avoid drafts
Make sure your kiln has cooled sufficiently before you open it. Hot brickwork and elements can be damaged if exposed to a draft of cold air, which will make them contract suddenly.

Do repairs
Repair all damaged brickwork. Elements will sag and eventually fall out of position if they are left unsupported because of defective bricks.

My elements always burn out at different times. Should I replace them individually, or all at once?

At low temperatures
When low firing, for bisque or earthenware (up to about 2010°F/1100°C), the kiln can often reach temperature even when one element is not working. In this case, you could replace elements individually, as they burn out, and still make full use of every firing.

When firing fails
When firing to stoneware temperatures of 2190°F (1200°C) or more – or if you find that your earthenware glazes do not fire properly with a faulty element in the kiln – you waste a firing each time a single element burns out. This could become expensive in wasted time and electricity, so it is better to replace all of the elements when one fails.

The elements in my kiln always seem to break at a critical time. How can I make an emergency repair?

burned-out elements break
the electrical circuit

rejoined elements create a
complete electrical circuit

Complete the electrical circuit
Before working on the kiln in any way, make sure you turn the electricity off at the main. To rejoin two elements that have burned apart, stretch and weave them together. Make sure the elements are touching so that a complete circuit is created for the electricity to travel along. The success of the repair will depend on this. Used elements are brittle when cold, so it may help you to heat the wire with a blow torch. Wear gloves that will protect your hands from the heat. This repair should last for several bisque or earthenware firings, but is unlikely to take the strain of stoneware temperatures.

Some of the elements in my kiln have started to sag, and snap when I try to push them back into position. What should I do?

Used elements are brittle when cold. To make any adjustments, heat them slightly with a blow torch or by turning on the kiln for a short time. Make sure the kiln electricity supply is turned off before attempting any repairs, and wear protective gloves. Elements usually sag because of gaps in their support, so repair any broken bricks quickly, before the elements drop out of their seating completely. As elements get older, they do not contract so readily, and sometimes fall out of place. When this happens continually, the only effective solution is to replace them.

I do not think all of my elements are working, but I cannot see any damage. How can I find the faulty ones?

Test the elements and connections

The fault may lie in the element itself or in the wiring connections, so you need to check both. Put a piece of paper on each element. Turn the kiln on for a few seconds. You will see scorch marks on the paper where the elements are working, as shown here. Carefully examine the elements that have not come

on to find any that have burned out. Next, examine the connections between the elements and the wiring of the kiln. It is possible that your elements are intact, but the connections have become loose or corroded. Refit any that look charred or doubtful in any way.

My kiln is taking much longer to fire than it should. What can I do?

Test and repair

Check that all of the elements are working. Replace any elements that have burned out, and repair any faulty wiring. As the elements age, they take longer to reach temperature. When this begins to ruin your glazes, or becomes uneconomical, change the elements rather than waiting until they burn out. Make sure that the lid and any bungs fit snugly, and that the brickwork or fiber is sound. You could be losing heat through gaps or thin walls, which will need repair. Be sure to pack the kiln as evenly as possible, as shown above. The heat will then be able to move around the kiln and reach all areas equally.

Chunks of brick have broken away from my kiln. Can I glue these back in place?

Repair broken brickwork with kiln cement bought from the manufacturers. It is specially designed to withstand the heat of the kiln. Ordinary glue or cement burns away or turns to powder and is ineffective for kiln repairs.

I am buying a secondhand electric wheel. What points should I look out for?

Check that you are comfortable sitting at the wheel, and that you can control the movement of the wheelhead with ease. Consider the size of the slop tray and how easy it is to empty; whether there is a convenient shelf for resting tools; and the overall size and weight of the wheel. Look out for a juddering wheelhead, or one that can be stopped easily in the hands while the wheel is on. This indicates worn bearings, and the price should reflect the cost of repair.

My wheel is making an awful noise. What can it be?

Check for clay
Check that the spindle of the wheelhead is free from dry clay and that the slop tray has not overflowed, as shown here. Clear your wheel of discarded clay more regularly. If the noise persists, have your wheel examined by an experienced wheel repairer.

I have done a small amount of throwing and would like to do more at home. Should I buy an electric wheel or a kickwheel?

A question of control
Many potters feel that a kickwheel gives them greater control, and you can certainly develop your skills on this kind of wheel. However, keeping the momentum of the wheel going, as well as concentrating on what your hands are doing, obviously requires more effort than using a wheel which keeps itself turning. Given the choice, most beginners learn on an electric wheel for this reason.

electric wheel

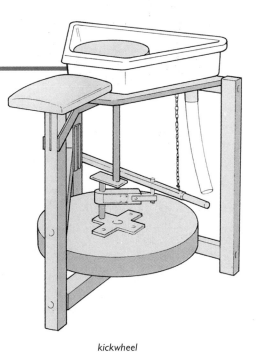

kickwheel

Clay continually sticks to my table when I am working. How can I stop this happening?

To prevent clay sticking, you need to find or adapt a slightly porous work surface. Tabletops made from wood, slate, or marble are a good choice. Where the working area becomes damp, dust it with a little talc or powdered dry clay. Laminated plastic is easy to clean, but clay sticks to it too readily. If this is the only surface available, you may find it better to place a wooden board on it, or to cover it with cloth – linen, canvas, or hessian are suitable. Choose a material which has an appropriate texture for your work.

I have a buildup of clay that is too dry to use. Do I need a pugmill to reconstitute it?

Reclaiming by hand

In large workshops where considerable quantities of clay are processed, pugmills quicken reclaiming. In a small-scale workshop, however, a pugmill is not necessary. Simply soak dry clay in a bucket and lay it out on an absorbent surface, such as a plaster bat, wooden board, or bisque trough, until it is firm enough to work with. Use a solid, flat area for wedging and kneading.

Is there any special equipment which would make rolling out clay easier?

Slab rollers make light work of creating large, even slabs. You can buy a roller to fit on a tabletop, or with an integral stand. An old-fashioned wringer makes a perfect slab roller, if you are lucky enough to come across one. Cutting through a large lump of clay with a harp is another way to make slabs. A similar construction formed from two sticks and a piece of wire will do the same job.

What equipment do I need to dry the wet clay or slip when reclaiming my clay?

Wooden boards and clay troughs

Cover wooden boards with a thick layer of newspaper and place some material on the top. Wet clay and slip can be laid on the material to dry, and the excess will soak into the newspaper. Keep replacing the newspaper as it becomes saturated. Bisque clay troughs, made by coiling or slab-building, are ideal for drying out reclaimed material.

Plaster bats

Use a wooden drawer or sturdy cardboard box to make plaster bats on which to dry your wet clay. Line the drawer with plastic so that the plaster will not stick to the sides. Mix enough plaster to make a bat at least 1½in (4cm) thick, and pour it in when runny, so that the surface is smooth and flat. When it has hardened, release the bat and round off any sharp or uneven areas with a surform or scraper.

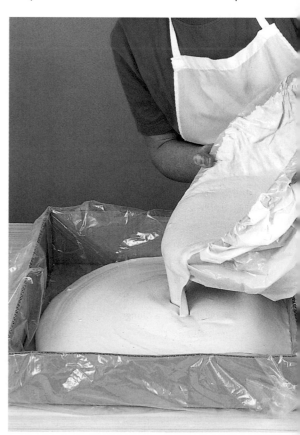

I need to see all around my work, so that one side does not become more heavily worked than others. What is the best way to do this?

Whirlers

Whirlers enable you to turn your work easily, and to see all around a pot without the risk of damaging it through continual handling. Even large boards can be set on a whirler as long as they are balanced carefully. Alternatively, prop up a mirror to reveal the reverse of your work.

I have been given some slipcasting molds, which I would like to use. Do I need special equipment to make casting slip?

Buy a blunger

For small quantities, it is easier and more reliable to buy ready-made casting slip from clay suppliers, as making casting slip without the proper equipment is a temperamental business. If you plan to make a large quantity on a regular basis, however, it is worth investing in a blunger, which mixes the clay slip from raw materials and keeps it at the right consistency. A slip pump siphons off the slip at the right pressure and de-airs it. You can also buy a specially designed workbench with troughs to catch excess slip and a series of wooden bars on which molds can be turned and supported.

How can I prevent the plaster from my molds contaminating my clay work?

Sensible precautions

Mix plaster in a bucket lined with a polythene bag. Any waste plaster can go straight into the garbage can inside the bag, leaving the bucket clean. Protect working areas by covering them with polythene, and utilize separate tools for plaster and clay. Check that the supporting walls of molds are secure, so that plaster does not leak onto work surfaces. Small molds can be placed inside a shallow cardboard box to catch any leakages. Take care to neaten the outside edges of the molds thoroughly to prevent chips falling into your clay. Round off sharp edges with either a surform or scraper, and sand down any bumps which may get knocked off during use.

My workshop is very small. What is the best system of shelving to use?

Shelving systems that allow you to adjust their height to suit your needs at any particular time are the best option for small workshops. Metal shelving units are also suitable, and work best with movable wooden boards, which give flexibility and compensate for warped metal shelves. Attach metals racks to the wall for stability.

The sink in my workshop gets blocked. How can I stop this happening?

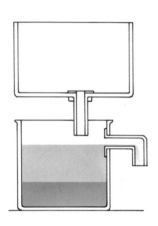

Use a claytrap

Installing a claytrap or sedimentation tank prevents sludge from blocking your drainage. The wastepipe from the sink runs into a container below. The pipe draining from this container is positioned near the top, allowing clay and glaze sludge to settle in the bottom of the container. Only water flows from the claytrap into your normal drainage system, and you can clean the sludge out of your claytrap at regular intervals. You may need to get a plumber to install the system.

How can I keep my pottery damp? I have no space for a damp cupboard.

Spray and wrap

Use a handheld plant spray to spray your pottery and the inside of a thin polythene sheet with water, then wrap the work in the polythene. Make sure that the polythene is tightly sealed by applying masking or parcel tape to any joins. Store in the coolest part of your workshop.

There are so many handheld tools in pottery catalogs, I don't know which to buy. Which are necessary?

Analyze your working methods

Decide which jobs you need a tool for, and exactly what you want the tool to do. Many tools have a specific function, such as turning, fettling, or decorating, so you can avoid those for which you have no use. Feel the weight and fit of tools in your hand. Some potters respond to the feel of wooden tools, while others choose metal because it is harder wearing. Only by trial and error can you find the tools that are best for you. New tools are being developed by manufacturers all the time. It is worth keeping up with new developments, but remain choosy about what you actually purchase.

I can only afford a few tools and would like to make more myself. What sort of tools can I construct easily?

Recycle everyday materials

Many everyday items can be commandeered for the pottery studio. Old toothbrushes, paintbrushes, and shaving and makeup brushes can be used for applying slip, colors, and glazes. Cut plastic credit cards, flower pots, and empty food containers into ribs for throwing and decorating. Fishing lines, model aircraft wire, and guitar strings make efficient clay-cutting wires. Worn-out carpentry tools, such as broken jigsaw and bandsaw blades, can be cut into sections to make loop tools; jagged hacksaw blades can be transformed into knives and scrapers. Hole cutters of varying sizes can be made from cut-down umbrella spikes, empty pen tubes, and drill bits.

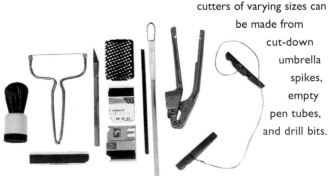

I often mix slip from leftover clay. How can I get rid of the lumps before sieving?

Useful equipment

A glaze mixer (shown here) will also mix bucketfuls of slip. A paint stirrer that attaches to an electric drill can disperse lumps in both slip and glaze. A kitchen hand whisk is useful when mixing small quantities of slip, but one used in the pottery studio should never go back to the kitchen.

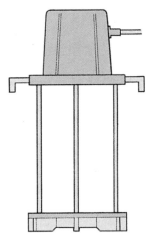

What equipment do I need in order to spray my glazes?

Customized sprays

You can buy equipment which is specially designed for spraying slips, glazes, and colors. Spray guns and airbrushes with compressors will give your work an even coating of glaze. Small, compressed air units are good for small-scale work. An extraction system and mask are essential for maintaining a safe environment while spraying.

Make your own equipment

A handheld plant spray, pump-action spray gun, or paint diffuser can all be used. These will generally not give as accurate a field of spray as equipment specifically made for the job, but they can create interesting results. You can make a spray booth from an old cylinder vacuum cleaner attached to a box. When turned on, the vacuum cleaner will suck the air and any sprayed particles out of the box.

Must I use a special spray gun for ceramics?

The materials used for ceramic glazes and slips have larger particles than inks and paints. Ceramic spray guns are designed to handle these particles; other spray guns may clog more easily. Grinding your glaze and slip materials finely will help them to cope.

What equipment do I need to grind materials?

Grinding manually

You can grind unfired or low-fired material with a pestle and mortar. These are usually made from dense, hard clay so that they do not chip or mark as the material is ground between their surfaces.

Grinding mechanically

Ball mills or jar mills grind ingredients very finely. The ingredients are placed inside the mill with ceramic beads. The mill turns on motorized rollers and the churning motion grinds down the material. Various sizes of beads are used to grind different types of material.

My tools have become very blunt. What is the best way to sharpen them?

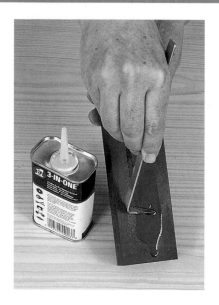

Manually or mechanically

The quickest way to sharpen tools is on a revolving grinding stone, holding the blade at an angle against the revolving wheel. These are usually available in larger workshops. You can also sharpen tools by hand, using an oilstone and oil. Squeeze a small amount of oil onto the stone, then rub the blade of your tool along the stone. Work in one direction only and hold the blade at a consistent angle. It may take some time before your tool is fully sharpened in this way.

I would like to mark my pots with an initial or seal. How can I make this?

Create a stamp or seal

There are many ways of marking your pots. Use rubber stamps on bisqueware, metal typeface on leather-hard clay, or make a raised seal, as shown here.

1. Draw your initials or design into a tablet of leather-hard clay with a knife or other sharp instrument.

2. When the tablet is hard, press a soft roll of clay into it, so that you form a reverse, raised image. Bisque fire your seal, and use it to stamp your leather-hard pots with your special mark.

I have a mask to wear during pottery making. When is it necessary?

Dusty jobs

Breathing in particles of dry clay and dust from glaze materials is the worst health hazard in the pottery workshop. It is good practice to wear a mask that filters out fine debris when doing any job which can create dust. Such jobs include fettling dryware; rubbing down bisqueware; making slip; incising dry clay; washing workbenches and floors; weighing and mixing glaze ingredients, oxides, or colorants; and sanding down glazes, oxides, or colorants. There are different kinds of masks. Those with changeable filters, although more expensive, are more efficient at filtering dust particles. These are called respirators.

How can I safeguard my sight and still see the cones when looking into a kiln at high temperatures?

Use a piece of colored glass or a commercially made cone viewer. Green glass is best as the iron particles that color it screen out the damaging infrared glare. Do not put your eye close to the hole, however, as neither of these protects you from the heat. Goggles that shield your eyes from the glare and the heat are the safest eyewear when viewing cones.

I would like to buy some clay for use in the classroom. What clays are easy for children to handle?

Use a general-purpose clay

The clay suppliers will give you a description of each type of clay, the techniques you can use it for, the temperature to fire it to, and the cost. Choose a general-purpose, inexpensive clay which is good for a wide range of techniques and does not have any special firing requirements.

Clays to choose and to avoid

Red clays can be cheaper to buy and fire, but are best avoided when working with young children, because the color from iron oxide is difficult to remove from clothing. A gray or buff clay does not stain to the same extent, and provides a more satisfactory background for color decoration.

I have clay in my yard. Can I use it to make pots?

Preparing your own clay

Clay deposits found in the soil can be made workable for pottery use, especially with additions of sand if it is too sticky, or a more plastic clay, such as ball clay, if it is too short. The temperature range of such clays is usually very low, so pots must be fired to low temperatures. It is generally preferable to use these clays in a glaze, where they can add unique qualities of texture or color.

1. Dig up a sample of clay and soak it in water until it is slaked down to a slip. Sieve all the debris and impurities out of the slip.

2. Lay the slip on a bat to dry. Once it is firm enough to handle, you can combine it with other materials to make a more workable body.

The clay that I am using is very old and has mold growing over it. Will it adversely affect my pots?

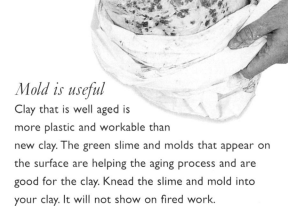

Mold is useful

Clay that is well aged is more plastic and workable than new clay. The green slime and molds that appear on the surface are helping the aging process and are good for the clay. Knead the slime and mold into your clay. It will not show on fired work.

Can I make my own clay from raw materials, and are there any drawbacks?

It is possible to mix clay from raw materials, and there are many recipes in pottery books for producing a variety of bodies. Although there are potters who make their own clay in order to create a body with particular qualities, others feel that the extra time and space needed for preparation does not make it viable. Even clay that is bought fully prepared from manufacturers is a relatively inexpensive material for craftwork.

My clay is very smooth and tends to slump when I am making large pots. Can I do anything to make it easier to work with?

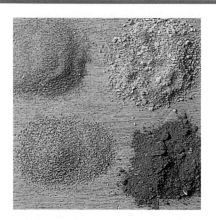

Strengthening additives

Knead molochite, grog, or sand into smooth clay to give a stronger, more open body for making large coil pots, slabwork, and sculptures. Choose from a range of differently sized and colored particles. Adding paper pulp to the clay will greatly improve its strength, but you may find it a little lifeless to use.

How can I give my work a heavily textured surface?

Creating clay with character

There are endless possibilities for creating textured effects. Wedge combustible materials, such as breakfast cereal, sawdust, rice, straw, or leaves into the plastic clay. These will burn away during firing to produce interesting holes and pockets in your work. Try rolling your clay onto textured material before using it to make pots. Corrugated cardboard, rubber mats, tree bark, lace, and frosted glass are just a few possibilities. Use slip to help create an interesting surface by pushing crumpled foil, broken brick, or other textures into a coating of damp slip. Alternatively, cloth can be dipped into slip and wrapped around a clay pot. Combine fragments of other clays, colored grog, particles of rust or glass, or other interesting materials with your clay to create a surface with character.

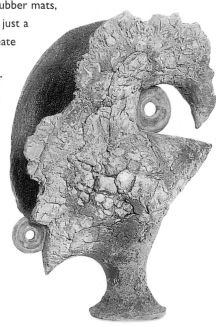

Right: Billy Adams,
Two-handled rock-a-billy pitcher

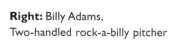

Can I make clay that I fire in an oxidized atmosphere look like reduced stoneware?

Use flecked clay

You can buy flecked clay bodies that produce a similar effect to reduced stoneware even when fired in an electric kiln. They contain particles of iron or basalt, which melt at stoneware temperatures to give a warm, flecked color. Alternatively, knead iron filings, rust particles, ilmenite, or basalt into an ordinary clay. This will also produce a richer color with speckles.

Can I do anything to stop my clay from shrinking so much?

The higher the temperature at which you fire your clay, the more it will shrink, and finer, whiter clays tend to shrink more than red earthenware clays. Changing your clay or your firing temperature may suit your needs better. Another solution is to add some grog. Grog is clay that has already been fired and has therefore already shrunk to some degree. If this material makes up part of the clay, the shrinkage rate of the whole will not be so great. Try wedging 4oz (110g) of grog into 2lb (900g) of clay as a starting point. Do not fire the clay beyond the temperature at which your grog was initially fired, or the grog itself will shrink, destroying the benefit of using this calcined material.

What is the best way to store clay, and how do I prepare for use after storage?

Plastic sheeting and airtight bins

Provided you use the clay quickly, you can keep it moist in its plastic bag, making sure that you seal it tightly after each opening. If you need to keep your clay for longer, pack the wrapped clay in a closed bin or in strong polythene sheeting. Store it slightly wetter than working consistency if possible to allow for drying during storage and preparation for use.

Dampen before use

If your storage space is warm, you may need to dampen the clay before use. Cut it into slices, and layer these in a bowl. Cover with water and let the clay soak until it has softened. Remove excess water by placing or kneading it on a plaster bat.

How can I dry my clay out quickly if it is too wet?

Place the over-wet clay on plaster bats, and turn it several times. This will draw moisture out of the clay. Then knead it until it is usable. Alternatively, knead dry, powdered clay into your plastic clay until you achieve the right consistency.

I find wedging and kneading clay very tiring. Is it really necessary?

Preparing your clay

Wedging and kneading clay removes air bubbles, and gives the clay an even consistency, rather than dry on the outside and wet in the middle. Make sure that you work on a table that is lower than your normal workbench, or stand on a platform to give you extra height. This will allow you to push down on the clay using your whole weight, making the process much easier.

1. To wedge the clay, pat it into a block and slam it down on the bench in front of you so that the clay lies at an angle. Make sure you work with an amount you can manage comfortably. The highest point of the block should be nearest you, with a gradual slope down into the table. Take a wire underneath the clay and make a cut halfway along its length.

2. Pick up the section of clay that is nearest and turn it so that the cut side is facing you. Slam it down onto the remaining section, and air will be squeezed out of the clay. Press the clay into a block again and repeat the slamming and cutting actions until air pockets are no longer visible when the clay is cut. When finished, pat it back into a rough rectangular block, ready for kneading.

3. Position the block with the short edges facing you. Using both hands, push the clay forward, away from you and down into the table. Immediately pull the clay back toward you so that it rolls back on itself. Repeat these two actions in a continuous movement. Note that kneading clay is not like kneading bread, which lets air into the dough. When performed correctly, the clay will form a spiral as it folds over and over itself, and all air will be removed.

I have lots of bits of clay which are too hard to use, and some broken pots which have not been fired. Can I make it all usable again?

Reclaiming clay

To reuse dried clay you must first soak it in water until there are no hard, dry lumps remaining.

1. Break the clay into small pieces and put it into a bucket with water. Start with some water in the bucket, so that you can be sure all the clay receives a soaking, then top up the water so that it covers all the clay. Let the clay soak until completely dry clay has disintegrated into a slip and hard clay has softened.

2. Drain off excess water lying above the clay, and lay the slip or soft clay onto a bat. When the clay has dried to a workable consistency, knead and wedge it. Good clay preparation is particularly important when using reclaimed clay.

My reclaimed clay is difficult to use and full of little bubbles when fired. Should I abandon reclaiming or can I improve the clay?

Give your clay a rest

Allow your reclaimed clay to rest for about six weeks before use. The clay often needs time to age before it regains its usual working properties. A few drops of vinegar in the water used for reclaiming assists this process.

Clay from a pugmill

It is often necessary to give clay that has been reclaimed using a pugmill a thorough hand-mixing to return it to a good working consistency. Wedge and knead the clay if you are having problems with little blisters or find the clay is no longer plastic enough to work with.

How do I make some slip for joining clay together?

Grated or crushed clay

You can use dry or leather-hard clay for making slip, or use the slops from a throwing tray. When joining pieces, you must do so with a slip made from the same clay as the original work.

1. Use leather-hard clay by grating it into small particles with a kitchen grater or woodworking surform.

2. Crush dry clay easily with a rolling pin or pestle and mortar. When using a rolling pin, place the dry pieces in a bag to keep the clay contained.

3. Mix the clay gratings or powder with water to form a slip. Hot water or a few drops of vinegar will help to break the clay down to a smooth consistency.

How can I make the clay I am reclaiming break down more quickly?

Clays which are particularly smooth, dense, and plastic break down slowly. Try using hot instead of cold water. Adding a little vinegar will speed the aging processes needed for successful reclaiming.

The pots I made yesterday cracked overnight. What happened?

Overnight frost

The most likely explanation is that your pots were affected by frost. The water in the clay has expanded on freezing, causing these cracks. You need to heat your workshop overnight sufficiently to stop the clay freezing in order to avoid this problem.

Do I need to use a special clay to make raku pots?

Raku pots are taken from the kiln while red hot. You can put pots made in any sort of clay into a raku firing, but clays that have a coarse, open texture will be more resilient to thermal shock and will therefore give you more success. You should expect a higher loss rate with clays that are smooth and dense, such as porcelain.

You can buy clays that are specifically made for raku work, but any clay with a high content of grog, fire clay, or other coarse-grained material will do. Wedge these materials into your usual clay body, experimenting with 5–20 percent grog, molochite, or fire clay. The shape and size of the pots you make are also factors in how successfully they fire. Large pieces require more heavily grogged clay than small bowls.

I would like to make flameproof ware. Is this possible?

It is very difficult to make pots which will withstand this type of cooking. A clay body must be very soft and open to survive the thermal shock of sitting directly on a source of heat. The shape of the pot is also important, so that no weak area occurs where the walls meet the base. Traditional red earthenware cooking pots used in many European countries are a good guide, with their rounded bases and open body.

What kind of clay can I use to make weather-resistant plant pots?

Vitrified stoneware

Plant pots intended for use outdoors can be vitrified stoneware. The water does not soak into these high-fired clays, and you can use glazes or slips to give color and decoration. You must be careful with the shape of these pots. An enclosing form will not allow any room for water to expand on freezing and this could crack the pot. Make your pots flare toward the top and have a wide, open rim.

Earthenware

Clay pots are traditionally made in red earthenware. Choose a clay that is sandy enough for building big pots, but does not contain grog. Any grog in the clay remains in porous lumps when fired, so that water can soak in and crack the pot in a winter freeze. Fire the clay to around the top range of its temperature, so that it is porous but not excessively so. This porosity is the reason why many gardeners favor clay pots over plastic alternatives.

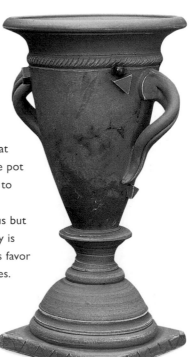

Right: Simon Hulbert, Red earthenware urn

I like porcelain because of its color and smoothness, but I find it cracks and warps easily. Can I do anything to improve this?

Add some molochite

Porcelain can become more workable with the addition of fine molochite. This gives it a slightly gritty texture and makes it easier to moisten for joining.

I. Use 8oz (225g) of molochite wedged into 4lb (1.8kg) of clay as a starting point, and adjust these proportions to your own preference.

2. Dampen the molochite with a little water so that it does not make the clay too dry.

3. Knead the damp molochite into your porcelain until well distributed throughout the clay.

Use paper pulp

Add some paper pulp to a porcelain slip and make into a plastic clay. The pulp will improve the clay's strength and its resistance to warping and cracking. If you find the paper fiber gets in the way of fine modeling, you can successfully work a layer of ordinary porcelain on top of the paper pulp clay.

How can I keep porcelain clean and uncontaminated by my usual clay?

Make sure that your working areas, such as wheel, workbench, and wareboards, are spotless. Clean and dry metal tools and brushes with metal barrels after use, so that they do not rust and contaminate the clay. If your work areas are very stained, perhaps from red clay, use a separate board for your porcelain. Work with separate tools, sponges, wareboards, and plastic wrapping if possible.

My porcelain pots are quite rough, but I do not want to glaze them. What can I do?

Smooth at every stage

Although porcelain is very smooth, it takes some work to achieve the silky surface for which this clay is known. Begin by smoothing the surface at the green stage with a fine sponge or paintbrush. Remove the roughness of sponge marks and fingerprints by sanding with wet-and-dry paper at the bisque stage, as shown below, and finish with silicon carbide paper when fully fired.

Is it possible to mix different kinds of clay?

Different clays can be mixed provided they are thoroughly amalgamated. If you are unsure what temperature to use for firing this new body, keep within the range of the lowest firing clay to be safe. If you want to make a piece that contains areas of different colored or textured clays, it is better to color and texture one type of clay than to use different types. Where clays of differing shrinkage rates are joined together, but not as a fully amalgamated body, the separate areas may pull apart as the piece dries and fires.

I use a sandy clay so that I can make large pots. How can I finish my pots to leave a better surface?

Wiping a heavily sanded or grogged clay with a sponge and water will draw the large particles in the clay to the surface. Smooth the clay with your fingers, a rubber kidney, a smooth pebble, or a rib instead. You can also cover the entire surface or chosen areas with a smooth slip, and transform the texture of the finished pot. Work made in rough, open bodies can scratch furniture, so be careful to grind foot rings and bases smooth, cover them with material, or stick small pads on the base to raise the work away from the furniture top.

I have heard about paper clay. What is it and why is it used?

Paper clay is clay that contains a proportion of paper pulp. It has very good green strength, amazing dry strength, and great resistance to cracking and warping. It is possible to join wet paper clay to dry paper clay without cracking, and even to make new plastic clay additions to bisque-fired work. The paper pulp burns away in the bisque firing, enabling the production of light, thin pieces.

Paper clay does have disadvantages. Many people find it unresponsive to work with. It is not possible to throw, pull handles, or model in fine detail, because the paper particles get in the way. Any paper clay left in a plastic state for more than a few days begins to smell as the paper rots, and firing paper clay creates noxious fumes until the paper burns away. Nevertheless, paper clay is a popular material among ceramic artists who wish to widen the scope of their work.

What sort of paper should I use to make paper clay and how do I make it?

Making paper clay

Use a type of paper, such as newspaper or toilet tissue, that will readily disintegrate into a pulp. You can use a food blender to hasten this process. Ready-made paper pulp, such as that used for papier mâché, is ideal. Use equal quantities of clay slip and pulp to make a very textured clay, or much less paper if a smoother clay is required.

1. Soak your paper pulp or torn-up fragments of paper in water until it disintegrates into a mush. Squeeze out as much water as possible and measure its volume. Add the pulp to your clay slip and mix thoroughly.

2. Lay the paper clay slip onto a plaster bat to get rid of the excess water. Use your paper clay as a slab straight from the bat, or knead it into a lump for use with other handbuilding techniques.

What other materials can I add to the clay to change its texture and properties?

Potters have been adding extra materials to their clay since Egyptian times, when fiber from bullrushes was used. Although pure clay became more prominent in recent history, there is currently a resurgence of using other materials in conjunction with clay as a way of widening the possibilities of the material. Experiment with fiberglass strands; fiber from coarse rope and matting; straw; cellulose fiber; powdered cement; material dipped in slip; metal shavings; and powdered plaster. You must be cautious when firing these materials. Do not fire in a kiln containing other people's work, which could be destroyed by your experiments. Test small pieces first to check for any extreme reactions and problems, and protect the kiln shelves by placing the work in a clay bowl. Begin by firing to low temperatures and make sure the kiln has an adequate extraction system to cope with any toxic fumes produced.

A white powder has formed on my red earthenware pots. How can I get rid of this, and what can I do to prevent it from forming again?

The white powder is salts from inside the clay, mainly calcium sulfur or chlorine, which have migrated to the surface. It is called efflorescence. Soak your pots in a solution of water and vinegar (in a ratio of 1:1) to remove the salts. Prevent the problem in future by kneading 1–2 percent barium carbonate into the plastic clay. Firing your pots to a higher temperature can also help.

I would like to apply slip to bisqueware when the work is easier to handle, but the slip will not stay on the pot. What should I do?

EARTHENWARE BISQUE SLIP

Calcined ball clay 35%
Calcined china clay 25%
Borax E frit 20%
Flint 20%

STONEWARE BISQUE SLIP

Calcined ball clay 35%
Calcined china clay 25%
Cornish stone 20%
Flint 20%

Use a special slip recipe
You must use a slip recipe designed for bisque-fired pots. This ensures that the shrinkage rates of the pot and the slip match. The calcined materials in these recipes are ball clay and china clay fired to 1830°F (1000°C). The same slips using uncalcined material will work on some bisque clays, depending on the shrinkage rates.

Increase adhesion with additives
Add wallpaper paste, acrylic medium, or gum arabic to your bisque slip to assist adhesion. Slip with these additions cannot be stored for more than a few weeks, and they may produce toxic fumes during firing, which will need extraction.

When I coat my pots with slip, they sometimes bubble and blister, or the slip cracks off. What is wrong?

Dampen your pots
The pots may be too dry when you apply the slip, and this is causing the blemishes. Try damping them with a spray – or better still, coat them in slip at an earlier stage. Make a slip from the body clay. This will ensure that the shrinkage rates of both body and slip are the same. Add a flux, such as a

frit, or a feldspar to the body clay to help the slip to fuse to the pot, and an oxide or body stain for coloring.

All the pots I dipped into slip collapsed. What did I do wrong?

Coating sequence
Coat the inside of your pots first, and let this dry fully before coating the outside. In this way, the clay will not become oversaturated and collapse.

Wall thickness
Make the walls of your pots thicker. Very thin walls are unlikely to stand up to the resaturation of a dipped slip. Try to form walls of uniform thickness, with no weak, thinner areas.

What materials do I need for making glazes?

To mix your own glazes, you need a range of powdered raw materials. These can include glass formers such as flint and quartz, which give a glaze its hard, shiny quality; fluxes such as frits and feldspars, which help the glaze to melt; clays such as china clay and ball clay, which help bind the glaze to the pot; and coloring and texturing oxides. These materials are weighed out according to different glaze recipes and mixed with water. You can also buy ready-made glazes in powdered form for mixing with water; in slop form for dipping, pouring, and spraying; or in a thicker consistency for brushing on.

What materials can I use to color my pots?

Use oxides and body stains for coloring clay and slip. Color your pots at the bisque stage with underglaze colors, glaze stains, and oxides. Use enamels, china paints, and lusters on top of fired glaze or vitrified clay.

When I color my slip with oxide or body stain, it looks washed out. Why is this?

Slip is predominantly clay and is opaque. The oxides and stains do not show up as they would in a clear glaze. You need more oxide or stain in a slip to achieve good color density: 5–10 percent of stain for a glaze, and 10–18 percent of stain for a slip. You may find it more satisfactory to settle for muted, pastel colors when working with slip than to try and attain the depth of colors available in glazes.

I would like to mix some colored clay. Can I mix color into plastic clay?

Incorporating colored paste

Mix color into plastic clay by making a paste from stain or oxide and water, and kneading this into the plastic clay. There is no exact way of measuring the amount of color needed, but good estimates can be made by carrying out tests of colored samples.

1. Weigh out four small balls of clay of equal weight. Measure 1 level teaspoon of colored stain, then measure three more quantities, using 2, 3, and 4 level teaspoons of stain. Alternatively, weigh the required amounts. Mix each measure with enough water to form a smooth paste, and knead each portion of colored paste into one ball of clay.

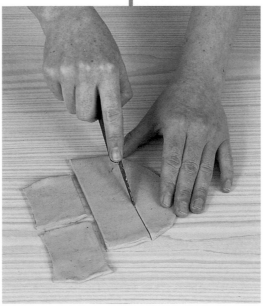

2. Make each ball of clay into several small slabs, and scratch how much color was used into the back of each. These are your test pieces, and when fired, you will have a series of slabs with progressively denser color. You can then see what different amounts of stain look like in your clay.

My colored clays bubble and bloat when fired. How do I cure this?

The coloring oxides added to the clay are acting as a flux and lowering the melting point of the clay. Turn the kiln off at a lower temperature to stop the bubbling. Another way of solving this problem is to reduce the amount of color you are adding, as bloating suggests an overload of oxide.

Which kind of iron oxide should I use in my recipes?

Choose by color

Unless stated otherwise, most recipes use red iron oxide, but it is possible to substitute this with another, such as black iron, crocus martis, and yellow ocher. Each gives a different color response.

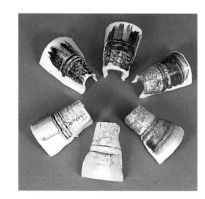

How much color should I add to slip that I already made up?

Calculate the dry weight of clay in a slip using either of the following formulas. If you wish to calculate the weight in ounces:

Dry weight of clay = $\dfrac{(\text{weight of one pint of slip} - 20) \times 2.5}{1.5}$

Or, if calculating the weight in grams:

Dry weight of clay = $\dfrac{(\text{weight of } \frac{1}{2} \text{ liter of slip} - 560) \times 2.5}{1.5}$

You can then add a percentage of that dry weight of body stain, which can be between 10–18 percent, depending on the depth of color desired. A simpler but less accurate way is to carry out tests using the same testing method outlined for coloring clay on page 37, using four equal amounts of slip rather than balls of clay.

All the recipes I have for slips, colored clay, and glazes use oxides. Can I use the carbonate form instead?

Use the following formulas to convert oxide to carbonate and carbonate to oxide:

$$\text{copper carbonate} = \frac{\text{copper oxide} \times 100}{65}$$

$$\text{copper oxide} = \frac{\text{copper carbonate} \times 65}{100}$$

$$\text{cobalt carbonate} = \frac{\text{cobalt oxide} \times 100}{63}$$

$$\text{cobalt oxide} = \frac{\text{cobalt carbonate} \times 63}{100}$$

Is it better for me to use prepared stains or oxides to color my glazes?

Smooth or textured

Although prepared stains are made from oxides, they contain a stabilizer, such as zinc or tin oxide, and are fired and finely ground, so that the color is smooth and more predictable than that of oxides alone. The consistent nature of stains is useful when you want a flat color, as shown here, but can seem dull when you want a textural quality. A stable color with some interesting textural qualities can be achieved by mixing stains and oxides. Rutile and titanium dioxide are particularly useful.

Right: Steve Mattison, Slip-decorated bowl

If I am using color as glaze stains and underglazes, must I buy two sets of colors, or are they interchangeable?

Interchanging glaze stains and underglazes

Mix underglaze colors with a little flux or clear glaze for painting on unfired glaze so that they melt into the glaze more readily. They can be mixed into glazes in the same way as glaze stains. You may need to add a little painting medium or glycerin to glaze stains for use as underglaze colors on green or bisqueware. This will help the color to flow as you are painting.

Right: Barbara Swarbrick, Rainbow lorikeets vase

Can I make my own pigmented wax crayons for coloring pottery?

Ceramic wax crayons

Use pigmented wax crayons to create colored areas that will resist a glaze. They have a grainy quality, much like using pastels on textured paper.

1. Melt two wax candles and ½ teaspoon of kerosene (paraffin) in a double saucepan or over a candle burner. Add an oxide or body stain to produce the desired color.

2. Prepare a slab of clay as a mold for your crayons by creating some hollowed out tubes. Mix the wax and color thoroughly and pour it into the hollows before the color has time to separate out. Release the crayons once the wax has set.

Can I make crayons and pencils for coloring pottery?

Chalks for drawing on bisqueware

The chalks and pencils sold for use on pottery are made from ceramic colors held in a binder. Make your own by mixing body stains and oxides with china clay, and firing them up to 1830°F (1000°C) until hard, or by using plaster as the binder, as shown here. Mix a small quantity of plaster and water in the usual way. Before it sets, add some color. Prepare a clay mold, and pour the colored plaster into the mold, to make tubes of color.

Can I make my own enamels and china paints?

You will need 85 percent lead or alkaline frit, and 15 percent ball or china clay. Add 1–10 percent glaze stain. Finely grind the mixture and sieve through a 150 mesh. Bind a few drops of oil or medium with the stain by working both together with a palette knife on glass. Thin with turpentine if necessary.

I love luster glazes but cannot reduce in my kiln. How can I get a similar effect?

You can buy lusters in liquid form to paint on. Fire them to about 1380°F (750°C) in an electric kiln. These lusters can be used on top of earthenware and stoneware glazes, but not all glazes are suitable. You will need to experiment to find a glaze which starts to remelt at just the right temperature to allow a reaction with the luster, but does not overmelt to spoil the luster design.

What is the best way to mend breaks in my dry pots?

Use vinegar

Scratch the areas that need repair and dampen them with vinegar. Mix some dry clay with more vinegar to form a paste. Smear this onto the wetted areas and gently push the pieces together.

Is it possible to mend cracks in bisqueware successfully?

Choose the right material

A crack in a domestic pot will always be a weak area, making the vessel unsafe for use. Such faulty pots are better discarded at the bisque stage. You can repair decorative and sculptural pieces, but cracks appearing during a first firing will often widen during a subsequent glaze firing. This is because stresses in the clay that have caused the crack are still present. On work which is not to be glazed, your repairs may be more successful if left until the piece is fully fired. You can then decide if the defects are small enough to make the piece worth saving. Miliput, stained plaster, and plastic padding make serviceable menders on fully fired clay. Experiment with one of the following methods to mend bisque work.

MAGIC MENDER

You can buy a magic mender or stopping from pottery suppliers for use on green and bisqueware. This can be stained to match your clay. Some products become shiny at high temperatures and affect the glaze adversely, but you can add some of your clay to achieve a more satisfactory color and texture.

MAKE YOUR OWN FILLER

Put a bowl of powdered clay into a bisque firing, so that the clay has been fired to the same temperature as the work and has the same level of shrinkage. Mix the powder with some flint and a flux such as feldspar or frit. Add water to make a paste. Press the paste into the crack. Leave to dry and then re-fire the work to bisque temperature.

USE PAPER CLAY

You can join plastic paper clay to dry or bisque-fired ware as a filler, and then re-fire your work successfully. Add wet paper pulp to a slip made from your clay. Let this dry to a plastic state and push it into cracks.

COAT WITH GLAZE

Fine cracks sometimes appear where handles and decorative features have been attached to a pot. These can be concealed by an opaque white or colored glaze. Brush extra glaze onto these areas to provide a good covering. Do not, however, confuse delicate, superficial cracking with structural defects which could cause an accident if concealed.

The casting slip I have bought is very thick. Should I add some water to make it more workable?

Casting slip is thixotropic, which means it will become jelly-like and solid if left to stand. You can make it more workable by stirring it. If it is still not thin enough, add a few drops of sodium dispex. Adding water will upset the balance of materials and will not improve the consistency of the slip.

Can I use ordinary clay slip as a casting slip in molds?

Casting slip is not the same as ordinary slip. It contains deflocculants, which allow more clay to be suspended in the water. Because the slip is denser, it dries more quickly in the mold and shrinks less. You can buy casting slip from clay suppliers, ready-mixed in plastic bottles or tubs. This is a wise choice if you do not have the right equipment for mixing casting slip, which can be a complicated and temperamental process.

Can I reconstitute the dried leftovers of casting slip?

You can use up to 25 percent of old casting slip in a new batch. More than this is likely to upset the ratios of clay and deflocculant. Soak your leftover fragments before adding to the new material. Sieve the slip to eliminate any unwanted lumps.

When I am making molds, how do I calculate how much plaster I need?

Experience
Most people underestimate how much plaster they need until they gain some experience. Look inside the walls you have built to contain the plaster, and try to calculate how much water it would take to fill the area. When you have made your estimate, use this amount of water to make up your plaster.

Make several batches
You can make a mold with several bucket-loads of plaster if it is large, or if you have underestimated your first load. Mix the second batch while the first one is setting. By the time it is ready to pour, the initial layer will be firm to the touch. Scratch crisscross lines into the first layer of plaster to act as a key to help the two layers bond together. Now pour your second batch of plaster and let the whole mold set in the usual way.

Is there a simple way of measuring how much plaster to add to water?

Floating islands
Each type of plaster has a ratio of how much weight of dry powder should be added to each pint of water. Ask your supplier to give you this formula. A less precise method is to sprinkle scoopfuls of plaster into a bucket of water. Move all over the surface so that the plaster falls in an even layer. Keep adding plaster until you are left with dry islands of powder which do not submerge. These islands tell you that there is enough plaster for the amount of water. Let the bucket stand for two minutes, to give the plaster time to soak into the water fully, then mix thoroughly.

As soon as we pick up a piece of clay to create a pot or sculpture, we must make choices about its size and shape. Decisions need to be made about color and decoration, and the important question of the pot's eventual function must also be considered. These are all elements of design, and it is by making our individual choices in each of these areas that we create pottery with a style and character of our own.

Form, Function and Design

I have no idea what shape of pots to make. Where do I start?

Look around you

Study the objects that surround you and that you use in your daily life, and you will begin to determine the forms that interest you. Look at pots in your home, in stores, museums, and galleries, and pick out shapes you particularly like. Bottles, bowls, and vessels made in glass, metal, plastic, and leather can stimulate ideas as well as those made in clay. If you are interested in buildings, transportation, lighting, or industrial items, they too can be a rich source of unusual forms and specific details to incorporate into your work. Observe the basic shapes of seedpods, vegetables, fruits, and flowers and use these to make pot forms. You can also translate the color and pattern of plants, animals, shells, or rock formations into decorative details.

Record your ideas

Keep a record of your ideas to refresh your memory when you work in clay. Use scrapbooks and sketchbooks to store magazine pictures, photocopies, photographs, and drawings, all of which can serve as source material.

I have been making the same shaped pots for some time. How can I extend my range?

Changing shape

Use your regular shape as the starting point for many variations.

1. Draw the shape of the pot on a piece of paper and cut it out to use as a template. Cut the template down the middle and across at the neck and the belly of the pot, so that you have six pieces.

2. Draw a base line on a large sheet of paper. Set the pieces of your template out, but manipulate the shape in one or more directions. Elongate the neck, make the base section taller, or widen the form, for example. Draw around each shape you make until you have a sheet full of ideas for new pots.

What are the main elements to consider when designing work to be made in clay?

The major consideration is that the work will eventually be fired. You must therefore learn to think ahead to avert potential problems arising from that process. Be sure that thick sections are hollowed and holes allow air to escape. Design any decoration or glazing as an integral part of making and not as an afterthought. You may need to plan for propping the work during firing.

Another aspect of working in clay is the unpredictable nature of the material. Firing can never be fully controlled. Even potters with years of experience can open their kilns to find that their preparations have not gone to plan. But these unexpected effects can sometimes be the most spectacular. Try to design your work with an open mind that will allow you to appreciate the surprises that may result.

I try to build pots that I have drawn, but without success. How can I translate my designs into clay?

Use a template

It can be difficult to translate a two-dimensional drawing into a three-dimensional pot. It is important to learn to see the profile of the pot, because that is the same as the drawing.

1. Draw the shape of your planned pot on a piece of paper. Divide it in half down the length, and cut out. Place the half pot on a piece of cardboard, and cut out the shape. This is your template.

2. Hold the template up against your pot as a guide. It will show you the points at which the walls should go inward and outward, and help you to shape your pot more precisely.

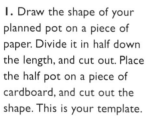

How can I use my computer to help me with my ceramic work?

An appropriate software package on your computer will enable you to draw designs for your pots. You can explore forms and decorative motifs, manipulate elements, and combine colors to produce a range of ideas to try out in clay. Three-dimensional models as well as two-dimensional designs are possible. There are also specialized packages that deal with glaze formulation, which you can find advertised in ceramic magazines. If you are linked to the Internet, you can consult information about galleries, exhibitions, magazines, materials, and equipment, and make contact with potters and artists from all over the world.

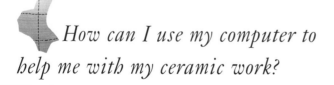

I cannot draw. How can I create designs for my ceramics?

Information recording

There are many ways of recording information that will help you to design your ideas for pots without drawing. Use photocopies from books, photographs, magazine clippings, tracings of designs, scraps of paper, and material that indicates color, texture, and pattern. You can also manipulate designs with the aid of computers and photocopiers.

Many people who think that they cannot draw find the task of recording what interests them very different from attempting a true-to-life depiction. The purpose of this visual recording is to gather information. It makes you study your chosen object closely and provides you with a means of remembering what you have seen. There is no right or wrong in these drawings. A small sketchbook, where you jot down notes, play around with ideas in a simple format, and record quick sketches is an invaluable personal source of reference.

Keep test pieces

Test pieces, made in clay and other materials, are also a useful way of collecting information. Recording the colors and textures of clays, slips, glazes, and decorative effects will help you to formulate ideas for finished pieces. Be methodical in noting how each test piece was achieved for future reference.

I have been making pots that are totally smooth and a little dull. How can I make more dynamic work?

Think about contrasts

Areas of contrast in the form or decoration give pots a dynamic appearance. Make textured parts stand out from the smooth surfaces, or apply busy decoration to contrast with plain areas. You can use color to follow the contours of the pot or to cut across the form in exciting lines. Vary the proportions of smooth and textured or plain and decorated areas: on one pot the pattern could be dominant, and on another it could form a special area of focus.

Above: Louise Darby, Pitchers with contrasting areas of decoration

Loosen your control

Think about decorating and glazing your pots in ways that are not totally controlled. Pour different colors of slip or glaze over a form, dip a pot into a color at angles, or use textured material or sponges to overlay designs. Let the materials work for themselves, and build on "happy accidents" to produce lively results.

Left: John Calver, Platter with poured and sponged glazes

How can I start to develop an individual style to my work?

It can be useful in the early stages to look at the work of other potters for inspiration. To move on from there and stamp an individuality on your work, you need to explore your special interests. Seek ideas from the world around you that you find stimulating and try to portray the essence of these in the building or decorating of your work, whether making functional pots or sculptural pieces. The shapes of fruit, mechanical objects, and architecture; the color and pattern in shells, flowers, and tropical fish; the texture of rock formations, rusting metal, and woven fabric; these are some of the countless sources that you can study. Experiment with methods and materials, so that you gradually build a personal way of using the clay. Look for focal points where you can make an individual statement, such as handles, lips, spouts, rims, and footrings.

The forms that I base on natural objects turn out to be very dead-looking. How can I give them some life?

Concentrate on aspects of the object that you find especially interesting. Make a study of such elements as shape, texture, color, or patterns of growth or decay. By using your skill and imagination to adapt these themes for your work, you will create forms with more energy and excitement than if you simply aim at a true-to-life representation of your chosen object.

When I wipe the glaze from the bottom of my pinch pots I am left with a messy edge. How can I make a neater finish?

Choose the right glaze

Use a glaze that flows very little or not at all. Then you need only wipe away a small area of glaze where the pot rests on the shelf, and this can be almost unnoticeable. Place a thin layer of sand underneath the pot to raise it from the kiln shelf during firing.

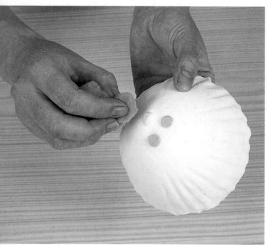

Give your pot feet

Make three tiny balls of clay and stick them to your pot in a triangular arrangement, using slip. After your pot is bisque fired it is easy to wipe the glaze away from the three feet, and leave the entire underside of the pot glazed.

Using trivets

Earthenware pots can be fully glazed and placed on trivets to raise them from the kiln shelf. The glaze melts around the trivet during firing, but you can break off the three points of the trivet to separate it from the pot. Sand down any sharp fragments after firing. Trivets can only be used at earthenware temperatures. Stoneware pots slump around the trivets and engulf them in clay.

I would like to make some very fine, elegant pots, but they turn out coarse and chunky. What is wrong with my designs?

The materials and methods you employ are important when trying to make finer, more elegant work. It is almost impossible to make very fine pots from heavily grogged clay. Coiling and slab building generally produce chunky pots, whereas slipcasting, pinching, and throwing allow more delicate work. There are two approaches you can consider. If you feel limited by your materials and techniques, change them to broaden your scope. Alternatively, concentrate on exploring the qualities of the materials you have and how you can use them to good effect, rather than struggling to achieve the impossible.

I am never certain where to put decoration or glaze on my pots. What can help me to be more decisive?

Plan for the decoration of your pot as you make it, otherwise any color or glazing can appear vague and unrelated to the form. Incorporate design features that set clear boundaries for decorative work. On thrown pots, for example, you can make lines as the pot is turning on the wheel to mark where a glaze or area of decoration is to end. Use a banding wheel or whirler in a similar way for coil or slab pots.

I have problems holding my pots for glazing. What can I do?

Plan ahead

As you make the pots, think about how you plan to finish them. Add features such as footrings that are not only decorative but allow you to hold the pot more easily. During glazing, you can hold a bowl by its footring and completely submerge it in the glaze in one action.

Decorative features

Plan the decoration so that areas are left unglazed and provide points where you can hold your pots. Double-dipping in two different glaze colors offers an easy solution.

1. Glaze the inside of your pot, and as you pour the glaze out, dip the top section of the pot into the glaze. Apply the outside glaze in an even line, or create a pattern by dipping the pot into the glaze several times at different angles. Your fingers are well away from the glaze and able to hold the pot firmly.

2. When the first dipping of glaze is dry enough to handle, hold the pot by the top section and dip the other end into a second color glaze. Dip it deeply enough for the second glaze to cover part of the first. The area coated with both glazes will become a third color when fired.

I have only one plain glaze. How can I make the best use of it?

Make strong forms

A plain glaze can be effective when the shape of the pot is the dominant feature, and no additional decoration is needed. Pots that have precise forms can be made in a series, so that their purity of shape becomes the focus of interest. This is not as easy as it sounds, and potters working in this way spend a great deal of time studying the proportions of their pots and the relationships of neck, rim, and foot to the body of the pot.

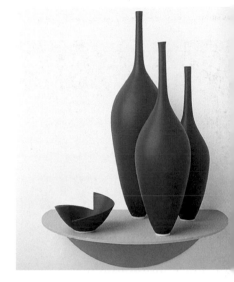

Above: Elsa Rady, Still life #52

Decorative effects

There are ways of decorating your pots that are particularly suited to a single color of glaze. Linear patterns and motifs that are incised into the leather-hard clay are greatly enhanced by a colored, transparent glaze. The glaze pools in the incised areas to add delicate shading. Opaque glazes can be applied to pots that are decorated with filigree work. Designs that are cut into the form or the rim of the pot need only a plain glaze as a finish.

Above: Peter Lane, Hedgerow bowl with filigree decoration

I want to make the decoration, the color, and the texture an integral part of my pot. How can I do this?

Left: Jo Connell, Urn made from colored clay

Choose the right clay and finishes

As you build your pot, use any indentations and textures left by your hands and tools to form a pattern. Work with colored or textured clay to incorporate decoration into the making process. Many glazes completely cover the clay and only provide a surface for design motifs. Choose finishes for your pots that enhance the color, texture, and shape, such as salt-glazing and flashings from smoked or wood firings.

Where can I find a source of patterns for my pots?

Keep a scrapbook of ideas

Our lives are filled with decorated material of every description. The problem is how to extract suitable motifs from this wealth of information. Begin a collection of decorative ideas that you find attractive. This can include magazine clippings, photocopies, computer printouts, scraps of material, wrapping paper, wallpaper, and greeting cards. Save combinations of colors as well as specific patterns. Once you have identified the styles of decoration that appeal to you, you can redraw patterns and motifs in your own style or make up new combinations to use on your work.

I want to decorate some areas of my pot and leave other parts plain. How can I test the best combination?

Create your designs on paper

Sketching your ideas on paper allows you to develop different patterns and color combinations and to choose the best one for your pot. Use a template to draw the shape of your pot many times on a piece of paper. If you are making a bowl, draw a circle for the inside as well as the profile. Alternatively, use a computer or photocopier to create the repeated shapes. Apply your ideas to the drawn pot shapes. Divide the pot into different areas, try out design motifs, and add different colors. Select the designs you like best for transfer to your pots.

I want to sketch my design directly onto my pot to be sure it will fit. How do I do this?

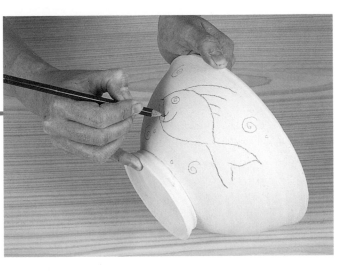

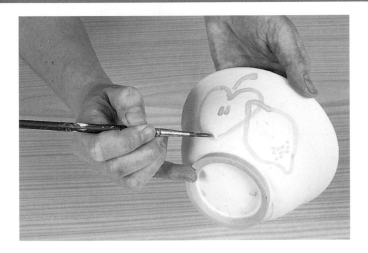

Using paint

A glazed surface is often too powdery to draw on with a pencil. Instead, use a pale watercolor, such as yellow or pink, which will fire out in the kiln. Strong colors, such as blue, brown, and green, may contain enough oxide to show in the glaze after firing. If you want to reposition a design, use a different color paint and ignore the first color. When you have placed your design satisfactorily, you can rework it with ceramic colors or glazes.

Using pencil

You can sketch designs on unfired pots using a soft pencil. Drawings can also be traced from thin paper or carbon paper by laying the paper on the pot and working over the back of the design with a pencil or pointed tool. Mistakes are easily corrected by wiping the unfired clay with a damp sponge. This will obliterate marks and smooth indentations to leave a clean working surface once more. When you are satisfied with your design, work over it with slip, ceramic color, or glazes.

Soft pencil is also useful for drawing onto bare bisque pots. Some crayons and colored pencils resist glaze and these should be avoided unless you wish to exploit an unglazed outline. The soft pencil lines disappear during firing, and mistakes can be drawn over or removed with an eraser.

When I try to draw a line down the wall of my bowl, the line always ends up slanting. How can I draw it straight?

Take account of the curve

To draw a line straight down your pot by eye, you must look directly at the position of the line. If you try to draw from an angle, the curve of your bowl affects the position of the line. Use a thin strip of cardboard, linoleum, plastic, or other flexible material to help you draw a straight line inside your bowl. Hold the strip so that it runs through the center point of the bowl, and draw along the edge to make a vertical line. When dividing the outside of the bowl into sections, remember that lines will come closer at the base, and widen out as you move up the bowl toward the rim.

How do I divide my bowl into equal sections for decorating?

A paper plan

There are several ways of measuring exact divisions on paper and transferring them to your bowl. A prepared paper plan allows you to measure bowls of different sizes.

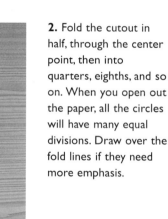

1. Using a compass and pencil, draw a number of concentric circles on a large piece of paper. Cut around the largest circle.

2. Fold the cutout in half, through the center point, then into quarters, eighths, and so on. When you open out the paper, all the circles will have many equal divisions. Draw over the fold lines if they need more emphasis.

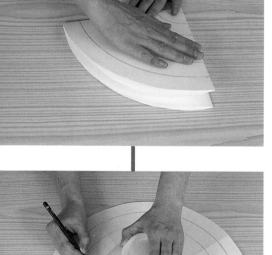

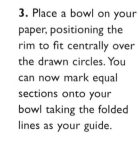

3. Place a bowl on your paper, positioning the rim to fit centrally over the drawn circles. You can now mark equal sections onto your bowl taking the folded lines as your guide.

A paper strip

Alternatively, use a strip of paper to calculate the exact divisions of one particular size of bowl.

1. Wrap a strip of paper around the rim of your bowl, and mark the circumference of the rim.

2. Fold the strip into equal sections to indicate an equal number of divisions. If you want an uneven number of sections, measure the strip of paper and divide the result by the number of divisions you require and fold accordingly.

3. Wrap the paper strip around the bowl again, and transfer the division lines onto the rim. You can now divide the bowl into equal sections for decorating.

How do I work out designs that are particularly good for sgraffito techniques?

Work with scratchboard

Sgraffito differs from most other decorative techniques, in that it entails scraping away color rather than adding it. Scratchboard – a cardboard coated with a layer of white clay and then a layer of ink, which is used by artists and designers – requires a similar technique. When lines are scratched into the black ink surface, a layer of white clay is revealed. This is therefore an ideal surface on which to plan and practice your designs for sgraffito work.

What sort of designs are possible using brushwork?

Left: Laurence McGowan, Albarello – stoneware pot

Above: Barbara Swarbrick, Diva – slab-built vase

All-over pattern

Use your pot as if it were a canvas, and draw a pattern or picture over the entire surface. The shape of the pot can add an interesting dimension to this decoration. Draw flowers, figures, landscapes, and abstract patterns freehand and leave them as linear brushwork or fill them in with color. Make designs to fit neatly into the surface area of the piece, or allow shapes to be cut off as if they flow beyond the edge of the pot.

Repeat pattern

Brushwork has traditionally been used to paint repeat motifs at intervals or forming a border around a pot. Producing a repeated design needs practice. Experiment with your chosen brush to become familiar with the shapes it can produce and the flow of color, and to gain confidence in your mark-making. Try painting your designs in wax, so that the pattern resists the glaze. Hot, melted wax is the traditional choice for this painterly method, but cold, liquid waxes are easier to use.

A single motif

Brush a single motif onto your pot. Designs painted in the center of a plate, or on one side of a pitcher, mug, or vase create a focal point. Commissioned work and commemorative ware relating to clubs, special occasions, and individual gifts often call for this kind of decoration. The more you practice your brushwork, the more confident and expressive your lettering and drawings will become.

Right: Andrew McGarva, Hen bowl – stoneware dish

My brushwork designs have become tedious and flat. What can I do to make my decoration more exciting?

Combine techniques

Designs that are totally planned can become static. Try incorporating a less predictable element into your decorating. Combining other techniques with your brushwork can result in unforeseen and attractive surprises.

1. Pour colored slips or glazes over your pots freely, so that combinations of color and background shapes occur spontaneously.

2. Work into slips with your fingers, tools, sponges, or fabric to create textural effects.

3. Apply your brushwork designs over this lively background. The combination of more formal elements on top of free-flowing color can give your work a fresh spark.

My pinch pots look as if they're grounded to the table. How can I make them appear lighter?

Give pots a lift

Raising the form a little will give the impression that your pots are growing out of the table instead of resting heavily on it. Three little feet formed from balls of clay can support the pot discreetly (above left), or be developed into decorative attachments that add to the organic quality of a pinched form. Or make a footring from a coil or an extruded or rolled slab of clay (above right).

I am making pitchers of many different sizes. Are some sizes more popular than others?

Think about how your pitchers will be used. Small pitchers can hold cream, yogurt, salad dressing, or sauces, and therefore a variety of sizes and shapes is useful. As the pitchers get larger, it becomes more important to know their capacity. Most people want a pitcher to hold a convenient amount, such as 1 pint (20fl oz/575ml) or 1 quart (1.2 liters), so that they can transfer a carton of milk or orange juice to it. Very large pitchers are usually intended for decorative rather than functional purposes, so the choice of size is aesthetic rather than functional.

How do I make a lip on a pitcher that will look good and pour well?

Shaping the lip

The lip is what singles pitchers out from other pots. Make it in a bold, confident way, and your pitchers will look more substantial and be more serviceable.

1. Make the rim of your pitcher extra thick, so that there is plenty of clay from which to pull out a strong lip. This will also emphasize the area where the lip and handle spring from the body of the pot. Thin the clay that is to form the lip by squeezing it between your thumb and fingers, and pulling upward. Pitchers that have thin pouring edges tend to drip less than those with thick lips.

2. Mold the shape of the lip by holding the rim at two points with the fingers of one hand, and working the clay area between with the forefinger of your other hand. Smooth the clay backward and forward with this finger as you pull it outward. It is important to create a large enough "well" in this way to enable liquid to be poured without spilling over the sides of the lip. Point the thinned edge of the lip downward to stop liquid running back into the pitcher when pouring is complete.

3. Run a finger or tool down each side of the lip. This tightens up the area of the rim where the lip pulls away from the pot and creates a bold visual statement.

I have tried to make pitchers that pour well by thinning out the rims around the lip area, but occasionally they still drip. What can I do to solve this problem?

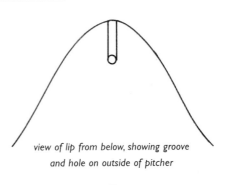

view of lip from below, showing groove and hole on outside of pitcher

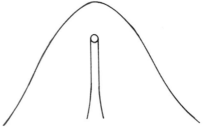

view of lip from above, showing groove and hole on inside of pitcher

Make a hole to catch drips

The most serviceable pitchers are made of metal, because the lips can be finely thinned without the edges chipping. The problem for potters is that an excessively thinned lip is a weak area that is liable to damage easily. The function of a pitcher must also be weighed against its aesthetic qualities. Most people who buy, use, and make pottery pitchers accept that these may be less efficient than their industrially made counterparts.

One way to tackle the problem of dripping, however, is to make a hole and grooves in the lip, as shown above. After pouring, any stray drops will be sucked in through the hole and down the inside groove back into the pitcher. Keep the hole open when glazing the pitcher, and wash it carefully to keep it clear when in use.

What shape of mugs are most practical to hold and drink from?

Above: Christine McCole, Stoneware mugs

Practical shapes

Mugs that are wide at the base will not be knocked over easily. Although a shape that flares outward from the base to the rim appears lighter and more elegant, you must weigh its aesthetic qualities against its functional drawbacks. Tapering or rounding the mug inward toward the top keeps liquid warm, but a final outward curve creates a more comfortable rim to drink from. Mugs with very thick rims are unpleasant to use.

 How can I attach the bottom of handles to mugs and pitchers in a decorative way?

Fishtails

A traditional attachment takes the form of a fishtail. Secure the handle with slip, pushing it gently onto the body of the pot. Working on one side of the handle, push the clay downward and outward, gradually smoothing it into the wall of the pot. Repeat this action with the other half of the handle, sloping it into the pot in the opposite direction. This gives the base of the handle a fishtail shape. You can continue to work into this area of clay to create a more elaborate feature. Use direct, vigorous strokes if you want a bold design.

Finish with a stamp

Once you have secured your handle to the body of the pot with slip, you can push a decorative stamp into the clay. Make stamps and seals by carving pictures and patterns into plaster, cork, and rubber, or by forming impressions in clay and bisque firing them. Create a design to complement your work, or use a seal of your initials.

How do I make handles that are comfortable to hold?

Comfortable handles

Remember that the clay will shrink in all directions as your mugs are fired. The width and thickness of the handle, as well as the distance between the handle and the mug, will become smaller, and you must make all these measurements larger than required when working the clay, so that they will be a comfortable fit when finished.

The position of the handle depends on the weight of the mug in use. If the handle is too low, the mug will feel unbalanced when full of liquid. Handles that sag as they dry also feel awkward in the hand. Make sure of a gently springing curve by turning your mugs upside down when the handles have been attached. Clay that is soft when damp can become sharp and unpleasant when fully fired. Neaten handles so that ridges and decoration present no sharp edges.

Right: Andrew Young, A well-rounded handle

How do I make a teapot spout that pours well?

The spout must be long enough to create a passage for the tea. Smooth any ridges on the inside of the spout that might disrupt the flow of liquid. Thin the tip and form a downward slope, as you would when making the lip of a pitcher, to stop drips forming. The area of holes in the body of the teapot must be greater than the area at the open end of the spout to ensure that there is enough pressure behind the liquid for smooth pouring. To prevent dripping after pouring, make a hole in the spout, in the same way as you would in the lip of a pitcher (see page 53).

The lids of my teapots always fall out when tea is being poured. How can I prevent this?

Creating a better-fitting lid

The simplest solution is to throw your lids taller. A lid with a very long flange can be slotted straight onto the teapot from the top, but the flange remains trapped when the teapot is tipped for pouring and cannot fall out. It is also possible to prevent the lid from falling by attaching a small piece of clay to the flange of the lid. This catches on the rim of the pot when the tea is poured. The disadvantage is that the snib of clay is vulnerable, and can be chipped or broken during use.

I have been making teapots with handles at the side. Are there any other unusual handles I can use?

Cane handles

Cane handles for the top of the pot are available from ceramic suppliers in several sizes. Make lugs from small coils of clay and use slip to attach them firmly to your teapot. Be sure to position the lugs correctly; they must stand across the spout and body of the pot for the handle to fit through the opening. Cane handles are often chosen to give teapots a Japanese or Chinese appearance, but you could also make your own handles from materials such as twigs, wire, string, or raffia.

Strap handles

You can make strap handles from clay that stand over the top of the teapot. Cut a strap of clay from a thrown ring or a rolled slab, or pull as with other handles. When the handle is firm enough to stand, attach one end where the spout meets the body, and the other to an area of the pot directly opposite. Look down on the top of the pot to check the alignment of the handle. Make sure that the lid fits in and out with ease.

I would like to make some lidded jars. How can I fit the lids?

Simple variations

There is an assortment of fittings to choose from. In some cases, the jars are plain and the lids have a more complicated shape; in other cases, the pots have a gallery into which the lids fit. The type of lid you require may be dictated by the function of your pot, but more often, the appearance of the lid is the deciding factor. The following diagrams offer some basic lid fitments, which give a starting point for designing lidded jars.

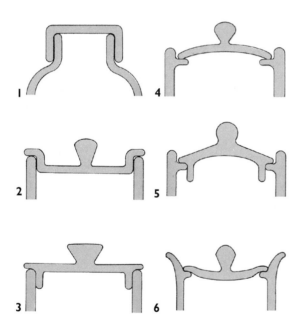

1. A cup lid fits snugly over the throat of the pot.
2. Use this lid when the maximum width of the pot is required. The knob can be incorporated at the throwing stage.
3. This lid can be used on pots with or without internal galleries.
4. A flangeless lid can sit on an internal pot gallery.
5. A flanged lid combined with an internal gallery is commonly used in articles where a secure fit is required to enable pouring, such as a teapot.
6. This lid is a simpler version of style number 2.

When writing on plates, how can I make sure the lettering fits?

Plan your lettering

Draw around the circle of your plate on a piece of paper and use this to plan out the size and positioning of freehand lettering. Transfer the finished design to greenware by tracing it through carbon paper or by drawing over the lines with a sharp tool. On bisqueware use the carbon paper method.

Cut-out letters

Use letters from a computer printout, photocopy, or instant lettering set to make paper resists. Experiment with a range of sizes, in lower and upper case, and with several styles to find the best fit for your plate.

1. Cut your chosen letters very precisely with a sharp craft knife. Arrange the letters on your plate in a suitable layout. Balance the spacing between the letters and align them to the curve of the plate. Stick the letters to greenware by wetting them and pressing them firmly onto the clay. A glue stick, suitable for paper and cardboard, can be used to stick the letters to bisqueware.

2. Apply color over the letters. Use a sharp point to raise the edge of each letter, and remove them before firing to reveal your finished design.

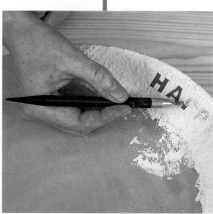

Make a stencil

Make your lettering a different color from that of your plate by cutting it out as a stencil. Print your design on a piece of paper with the help of a computer or other cut-out letters. Once you are sure that the lettering will fit your plate, cut out the individual letters, using a sharp craft knife. Place the stencil over your plate and sponge or brush colored slip, glaze, or oxides into the cut-out areas. This will produce your entire design – on your plate.

The plates I make are awkward to eat from. What design elements will give me a more serviceable plate?

Making a plate

One problem that can occur with handmade plates is that they can be too flat. When you throw or roll out a plate, check that there is enough depth to allow fingers to move underneath the rim and lift the plate up. Create an area in the center of your plate that is either flat or slightly concave, but never convex. Consider the proportions of the rim and the body of the plate, and whether the rim is a decorative feature or is necessary at all. An inexperienced thrower often makes plates that are too heavy for their size. Practice turning away excess clay from the base of your plates until you achieve a more suitable weight.

How do I begin making functional items that perform well?

Study other functional items

A good way to start is to study items that you use in your home and that you see in stores. Consider the ways in which these items perform well, and how they might be improved. Look at objects made in metal, glass, and plastic, as well as factory-made ceramics and handmade pottery. You will probably conclude that function is not the only consideration in your work. How pots feel and how they look are also important aspects for most potters – and for most users of handmade pots.

Right:
Jonathan
Keep, Teapot

I want to make some differently shaped pots that form a set – a mug, bowl, and plate, for example. How can I create a link between them?

A set of ceramic pots, however limited or extensive, must contain similarities despite its members' varying shapes. Your own style will almost certainly reproduce certain elements in all the pieces you make. The thickness of rims, the proportion of smooth and textured or plain and decorated areas, and the basic shape of the pots (chunky, elegant, angular, and so on) will create a simple unity. Give handles, rims, or feet a particular style of decoration or distortion to provide the pots with an additional link. An interesting aspect of designing sets of pots is that any decoration – single motifs, combinations of color, or patterned borders – must be manipulated to fit the curves of a bowl, the rim or flat area of a plate, and the cylindrical shape of a mug, vase, or pitcher. Experiment with designs drawn on paper, or on a computer.

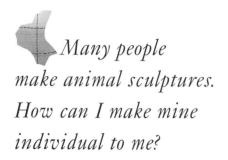

Many people make animal sculptures. How can I make mine individual to me?

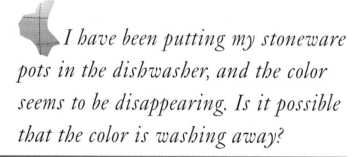

Left: Gill Bliss, Cockerel

Creating a style of your own

Carry out a close study of the animals you wish to sculpt, using photographs in magazines and books, videos, television programs, and if possible sketches from life. Note the characteristics of each animal that particularly intrigues you. It may be the overall form; the way an animal moves; how it curls up when asleep; the colored markings that run through its coat; the animal's temperament; or its reactions when frightened or hunting. Focus on these themes and try to express them strongly through your work. As you build with the clay, look for techniques, colors, and textures that help to express the qualities you want to portray.

I have been putting my stoneware pots in the dishwasher, and the color seems to be disappearing. Is it possible that the color is washing away?

The color cannot be washed out of a high-fired glaze. It is more likely that the dishwasher detergent is affecting the surface of your pots and making the color cloudy. Regular dishwasher detergents are very abrasive and can damage a glazed surface. Use a product that is specially formulated for delicate items, or wash by hand if you do not want to risk damaging your special pots.

If the colored decoration on your pots is low-fired enamel, it will not withstand the rigors of mechanical dishwashing. Enamels are not part of the glaze; they sit on the surface, and they are rubbed away by repeated washing in a dishwasher.

What sort of glazes should I use on functional ware?

Glazes for use on functional ware are generally shiny or silky and very hardwearing, so that items can be washed efficiently and withstand continual cutlery use without marking. Crazing is a problem, even on vitrified stoneware or porcelain, because food particles and stains creep into the cracks, making unsightly dirty lines. A crazed glaze on earthenware renders the pots porous.

Pots that are used to hold food should have a well-balanced glaze coating. Glazes that are formulated with an overload of materials such as barium or coloring oxides are unstable, and particles may leach into food. Although lead frits are manufactured to render them safe for functional glazes, you must use them in a suitable glaze formula. Never use copper with a glaze containing lead. Cadmium, which is the colorant in many bright red glazes, must not be used inside pots intended for food. If you are unsure about the safety of your glazes, ask your ceramic supplier for information about testing them in laboratory conditions.

Should I make clay plinths for my work? How can I know if this would improve the pieces?

Question its suitability

Ask yourself the following questions: Does your work need a plinth for stability? Would a plinth hold together several parts to unify the work? Would a base add a new dimension or more information to the piece? Questioning the suitability of a plinth in these ways should enable you to recognize whether it will enhance or detract from your work.

Above: Christine Derry, The forest of philosophers

I would like to make plinths for my sculptures but not in clay. What other materials do you suggest?

Suitable materials for mixed media

Wood, slate, metal, resin, plaster, and marble are some materials that have been used successfully with ceramic. Choose a material that will enhance your sculpture and not overwhelm it. The color and texture must not distract the eye from the main body of the work. The relative proportions of the plinth and the sculpture are important. In some cases a small base is appropriate, and in others a plinth that is larger than the sculpture itself can focus the eye more accurately.

Left: Andrea Hylands, Cyclolites

I usually make small sculptures that will fit onto a shelf easily. Do you think large-scale sculptures are more impressive?

We are all used to living with objects of a domestic scale that sit on shelves and tables and do not dominate the space in a room. Art and craftwork of a larger size is viewed differently because it is not generally such an integral part of our daily lives. Miniature pieces can also attract attention because of their unusual size. Representing objects in other than their normal size can be a way to create striking images.

The dimensions of the work must accord with the ideas that are being expressed. Sometimes sculptures that look right at the maquette stage, when relationships are being worked out on a smaller scale, become lifeless or unbalanced in the final, enlarged work. You can only find the appropriate scale for your sculptures by trial and error. It is by no means true that all large-scale work is good, or necessarily better than sculptures of lesser dimensions.

It is much easier to find a home for domestic-sized pieces. If you plan to produce larger items, you need to consider where these might be sited. Outdoor sculptures, for example, must be weather-resistant. This sort of consideration can affect your materials and techniques.

CLAY IS A tremendously versatile material. We can use our

hands to pinch or coil it into organic shapes, or we can use

slab-building techniques to produce angular constructions

from firm sheets of clay or flowing forms from softer slabs.

Many potters discover an affinity with one particular

method, but you can also combine techniques to open up

further possibilities for exploring original ideas.

Handbuilding

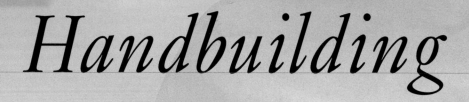

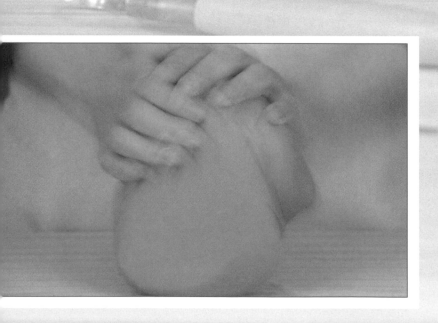

My pinch pots are lopsided and uneven. How can I make them more symmetrical?

Use clay of an even consistency
Any hard or soft lumps in the clay make pinching irregular. Pat the clay into a ball between the palms of your hands and smooth over any cracks that appear. This will give a good start to your pot.

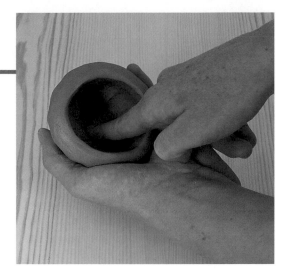

Use your thumb
You cannot build a symmetrical pot if there is more clay on one side than the other, so push your thumb straight down into the center of the ball of clay. Turning the ball as you insert your thumb will help to make the opening more central.

Use a range of shaping techniques
Although this method of building pots in the hand is called pinching, there are other movements apart from squeezing that you can make. These help you to control the shaping of your pot. Hold your pot in one hand and smooth out the inside with the fingers of the other hand. Work from the bottom of the pot to the rim, and you will find that the walls grow and shape against your palm.

My pinch pots are heavy and lumpy. What can I do to get smooth and regular walls?

Make a thin base
Avoid excessive weight at the base of your pots. Push your thumb far enough into the ball of clay to leave only a thin base, and begin squeezing at this point.

Work slowly
Do not attempt to thin walls quickly. Shaping gets out of control if you squeeze the clay too hard. Work slowly, a little at a time, so that you can build up a regular rhythm of pinching and turning.

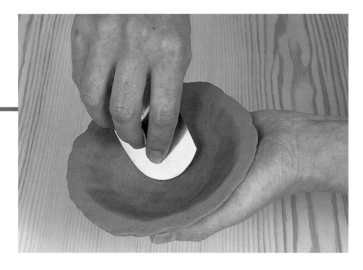

The finishing touch
Finish shaping your pots with a rubber or metal kidney. Scrape both the inside and outside of the pots with the kidney when they are leather-hard, to remove irregularities.

The rims of my pinch pots always start to crack. How can I stop this from spoiling my work?

Keep the rims malleable

To prevent cracking, leave an extra thickness of clay at the rim of your pot. Work on the rim last, so that the clay is soft and fresh, and keep the rim damp by moistening with a sponge and water. Do not, however, wet the entire pot, or it will become sticky and slippery to work. Alternatively, encourage and accentuate irregularities at the rim so that the cracking and folding clay gives an organic quality to your pinch pots.

I want my pots to have neat rims. What must I do to achieve this?

Cut and smooth

Cut away irregular rims to give a better finish to your pots. Working on a whirler will help you to make a straight cut. Score all around your leather-hard pot and cut along the line with a sharp knife. Smooth sharp edges away with a damp sponge.

Add a coil of clay

The extra thickness of a coil at the rim contributes a bolder finish to the pot. Scratch and slip the rim of your leather-hard pot, and attach a coil which is slightly thicker than the walls (left). Smooth the coil into the pot on both the inside and outside (below), but do not squeeze the coil too thin.

My pinch pots always turn into flattened dish shapes. How do I extend the walls without pushing them out too far?

Use the right shaping technique

Making pots by pinching is not as easy as it might initially appear. You will need patience and perseverance to learn this technique. Squeezing too much clay at a time causes the pot to lose shape, so rest your pots before they become overworked and floppy. Build more than one at a time, so that each has the chance to harden a little.

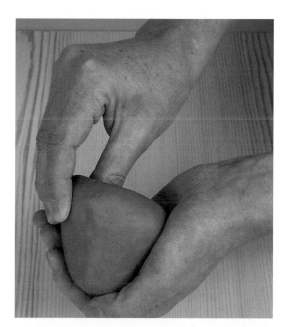

SUPPORT WITH YOUR HANDS
Always work with the pot in your hand and never pushing down onto your workbench. Cup your palm to provide a rounded seat for your pot. Squeeze slightly around the circumference of the pot with the hand that is holding the pot.

A COLLARING ACTION
Gently squeeze your pot inward with both hands when it spreads too wide. This is known as collaring. Turn your pot to repeat this action all the way around its rim.

I join pinch pots together to form a wider range of shapes. What is the best way of attaching the rims?

Clay of equal consistency

Join pinch pots by scratching the rims and applying slip in the usual way. Make sure that the rims are of equal thickness and both pots have dried to the same extent. The shrinkage rate for both pots will then be the same.

Stuff your pots

Filling your pots with crumpled newspaper gives you a firm surface to press against and helps you to make a secure join.

1. Pad both pots with balls of crumpled newspaper. It will burn out during firing.

2. You can now smooth over the seam where the two rims join without distorting the shape of your pot.

Slope rims outward

Form outward-sloping rims on the pots you wish to join. Pots with inward sloping rims will always have a weakness at the seam.

I dry my pinch pots on a wooden board, but this flattens their bases. How can I prevent this from happening?

Coil supports

It is better to place your pots on a cushion of soft material than a hard tabletop. Use coils of clay to make a variety of rings for your pots to sit in. You can then select a suitable ring for each pot.

Ready-made supports

Keep a selection of bowls, cups, and cylinders handy to hold the pots during resting or drying. Use pieces of foam, wadding, or paper to pad the hard rim of a supporting vessel. Alternatively, rest your pots directly on a soft surface, such as foam, crumpled newspaper, or wadding.

I want to give my pinch pots some lift. How can I make footrings for them?

Coil footring

Make a footring from a coil of clay for a gentle lift.

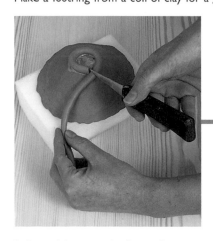

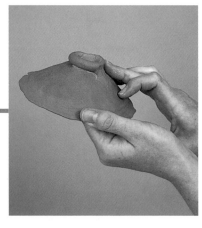

1. Scratch lines on the base of your pot with a sharp knife. Coat this with slip to give a sticky area where the footring will join. Push a coil in place and cut to size.

2. Use a finger to smooth the coil into the pot to form a secure join. Finish by neatening and shaping your footring with a damp sponge.

A cylinder footring

A small cylinder of clay will create a taller footring. Cut a strip from a rolled-out slab of clay. The width of this strip is the height of your footring. Form the strip into a cylinder of the desired size, and join the cylinder to your pot in the usual way, taking care to smooth over the seam with a finger or wooden tool. Neaten with a damp sponge to finish.

How can I introduce color into my pinch pots?

Using colored clays

Pinch pots have an organic, flowing form, and color should enhance this. You can buy a selection of colored clays from your supplier, or mix them yourself, using stains or oxides and a light-colored body. Twist and knead several colors of clay together and form into a ball. The color flows through your pot as you pinch out the walls.

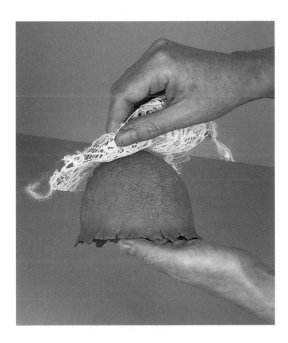

Pattern your pots

Use color to emphasize textured surfaces on your pots. Make a collection of materials, such as lace, leaves, and twisted cord, that will make interesting patterns. Press textured material into the surface of your pot with the help of a spoon, tool, or smooth pebble. You may need to dampen the walls of your pot a little for the pattern to transfer well. Paint the dry or bisque-fired pot with a stain or oxide mixed in water. When dry, wipe over with a damp sponge to reveal a delicate tracery of color.

A marbled effect

Knead some stain or oxide powder into your plastic clay. The veins and specks of color will give your pot the appearance of marble.

1. Sprinkle powdered color onto a slab of clay and roll together. Knead the clay and shape into a ball, ready for making your pots.

2. As you pinch the walls of your pot, the color pushes through the clay in streaks and veins.

Colorwash rims

If your pots have cracked and folded rims, enhance them with color.

1. Paint an oxide or stain onto the rim of a dry or bisque pot, making sure the color goes into the folds and wrinkles of the clay.

2. Wipe over with a damp sponge. The color remains trapped in the crevices of the clay and highlights the organic rim of the pot.

My clay coils always go flat or begin to flake apart. What can I do to improve my technique?

Use soft clay

Clay loses moisture quickly because of the warmth from your hands. When it is too hard, it cracks, forming air pockets that make it impossible to work. Start with clay as soft as it can be without sticking to the table.

Delay rolling

Begin making a coil by shaping a lump of clay into a sausage. Keep squeezing the sausage until it is almost the width you require. Delay rolling it for as long as possible – just carry on working the clay into a thinner sausage. Finally, roll your coil only as a way of finishing the shaping.

Apply the correct pressure

Flat coils suggest that you are putting too much forward pressure on the clay as you roll. Try to stretch the clay outward with your rolling action instead. Move your hands sideways, along the length of the clay, as well as in a backward and forward motion, as in the sequence shown above. Check that you are rolling all the way around the clay and back again on each roll to prevent the coils from becoming flattened. Do not make your coils thinner than finger width, or they will not contain enough clay to make strong walls for your pot.

Is it possible to make coils with a special tool rather than always rolling them out by hand?

A coiler

A coiler tool is designed to slice a coil out of damp clay. A loop of wire can be used instead. Run the wire or coiler down the length of a well-prepared block of clay to produce an even coil.

Square sections

Cutting strips from a slab of clay gives you square-shaped coils to use in the same way as round coils. Roll out a slab of clay, using thick wooden guides. Use the width of one of the guides to measure strips of clay.

Extruded coils

You can make a large number of coils using a machine known as an extruder, or wad box. You feed clay into the machine and pull a lever to force it through a shaped template and out in the form of a coil.

The bases of my coil pots always crack. How can I prevent this?

Roll out bases

Do not coil your bases. The coils sometimes separate in the firing. Cut your bases from a rolled or patted slab of clay. You can use a lid, pastry cutter, small bowl, or jar as a template to help you cut a circle.

Pots of even thickness

Try to make the base and walls of your pots the same thickness. Bases that are much thicker than walls take longer to dry. Stresses caused by the uneven shrinkage can cause cracks.

Turn your pots over

Dry the bases of your pots thoroughly before firing. Clay that is still damp when fired tends to split. Turning your pots upside down helps the bases to dry completely.

Build on paper

The pressure of building may be sticking your pot to the table, causing the base to split when the pot is moved. Try building your pot on a piece of paper.

The walls of my coil pots get progressively thin and eventually collapse. What am I doing wrong?

Effective joining technique

When learning to coil, many people try to join the coils together by squeezing the clay between fingers and thumbs. This action cannot join the coils adequately and causes excessive thinning of the walls. The following technique will make your coiling more effective. If you have difficulty doing this technique with your fingers, you may find a wooden tool useful.

1. Attach a new coil by pushing some of the clay from this coil down into the clay of the pot. Work around the inside, sealing the seam between the new coil and previous work.

2. When the inside of your pot is smooth, join the outside of the coil in same manner. This secures the coils together, but leaves the majority of the coil standing to form a solid wall.

If I need to leave a coil pot half-finished, how should I store it until I can work again?

When I have left a pot for a while, do I need to prepare the clay before I start work on it again?

Keep work damp

You must make sure that the clay remains damp enough to give you a good working consistency when you return to your pot.

1. If you are leaving your pot for a few hours, you need only attend to the rim. Spray the pot lightly with water, or wet the rim with a damp sponge.

2. Next, wrap a damp cloth around the edge of your work, or cover it loosely with either plastic cling wrap or a sheet of polythene.

3. If you are leaving your pot for several days, you must seal it away from the air to keep it damp. Spray the pot lightly with water and wrap it carefully in plastic. Make sure you exclude as much air as possible, and tape the plastic in place.

Scratch and moisten

If the top layer of clay has stiffened at all, you must treat it before joining the next coil.

1. Score the rim of your pot with a knife or needle. This opens the clay to receive the moisture. Wet the rim with a sponge, allowing the water to soak into the clay, then brush on some slip.

2. Your pot is now ready to add the next coil. Smooth the coil into the walls of the pot on the inside and then the outside edge, in the usual manner. Sometimes a ridge forms where a new session of work began. This can easily be smoothed out with a rib.

I do not seem to have much control over the shape of my coil pots. How can I make my pots the shape I want?

Use shaping techniques

The key to control of your coil pots is to understand the methods of shaping. Once you know what makes the walls come in or go out, you can be more exact in the forms you create.

OUTWARD SHAPING

Apply a new coil to the outside of the previous coil to make the walls swell outward. The form becomes wider – when making the belly of your pot, for example.

INWARD SHAPING

Add a new coil to the inside of the previous coil to make the walls slope inward. The form becomes narrower – when closing toward the neck of your pot, for example.

ONE STEP AT A TIME

Work on one coil at a time. If you wind up lots of coils before starting to join them, it is very difficult to control their shaping. Cut off each coil after one circle of the pot.

FORWARD PLANNING

Have a clear idea of the pot you want to make before you begin. This helps you to make the necessary shaping in a decisive way. Keep a sketch close at hand while you work.

Sometimes a coil pot I am making suddenly begins to sag. Everything I do makes it worse. Why is this happening?

Allow time for clay to stiffen

Give your pots a rest before they sag. The walls of coiled pots support more and more weight as work progresses, and unless the clay is given time to harden a little during building, it will begin to sag, as shown here. It is good practice to have several pots at different stages of making, so that you can move from one to another, allowing each to have a rest period when necessary.

My coil pots look lumpy and uneven. How do I make them more symmetrical?

Work in the round

It is easier to keep your pots symmetrical if you can see and work all the way around them. Move the pot while remaining in a stable position yourself, or keep the pot still, and go around it as you work. The easiest way to turn your pot is to use a whirler or turntable.

Build in circles

Join your coils in one complete circle at a time. If you carry coils over from one layer to the next, it is more difficult to keep the pot symmetrical.

Shape with a rib

Use a rib to consolidate the clay and improve the shape of your pots. You will find that working over your pot with a rib after several coils are added helps to tighten up the form.

I love the shape of the pots I get from coiling, but don't like rolling coils. Is there any alternative method?

Extended pinching

Make your pots by the extended pinching technique. This uses lumps of clay instead of rolled coils.

1. Squeeze a piece of clay in your fingers to form an even thickness. Attach the clay to your pot, and extend the walls by pinching and squeezing it. Be careful to make the walls grow upward and not always outward.

2. Smooth over the inside and the outside of the pot to make a good seam. You are now ready to attach the next piece of clay.

Build in sections

This is a very quick way of constructing walls, but needs some practice to control the shaping of your pots.

1. Roll out a slab of clay and cut this into wide sections. Use the strips to build up the walls of your pot.

2. Join the seams very carefully, since these will be the weakest areas of the pot. A rib will help you to shape the walls further. You may need to rest the pot each time you join a section, to allow the clay to stiffen.

How do I make slabs of even thickness?

Choose the correct clay consistency

Soft clay is easier to use if you are rolling out your slabs. You can then let it dry after the hard work of rolling is done. Stiff clay is preferable when cutting slabs from a block with a harp. If you use soft clay for this method, the slabs will not retain their shape.

Using a slab roller

A slab roller makes light work of large slabs. The heavy roller moves along the table, flattening the clay to a preset thickness. A cloth is usually included on which to roll the clay, so that it is easy to remove it for further working.

Cutting even slabs

Cut slabs from a stiff block of clay with a harp, or make a similar tool from two wooden sticks and a wire.

A rolling pin

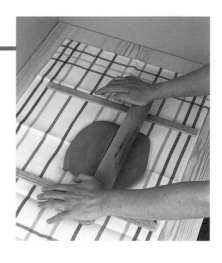

Use a rolling pin and two strips of wood to serve as guides. The guides must be of equal thickness and long enough to stretch the full length of your rolled-out slabs. Place a chunk of clay between your wooden guides, and roll it flat. When the rolling pin touches the wood along the complete length of a roll, you know that the clay is the same, even thickness as the guides.

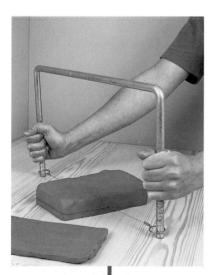

1. Position a block of stiff clay on your work surface, and cut a slice from the bottom of it. Press the two arms of the harp firmly down against the tabletop to maintain an even thickness. If you use your own cutter, remember to keep the wire taut while slicing.

2. Place your hands along the sides of the block of clay, and lift it away from your first slab, onto a clean area. You are left with an even slab of clay. Cut more slabs in the same way from the remaining block of clay.

 When I roll out the clay, air bubbles sometimes appear. What is the best way to get rid of these?

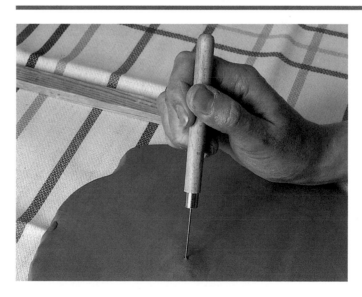

Prick the bubbles

Release the air in your clay by pricking bubbles with a needle. Squeeze the air out and smooth over the clay before re-rolling. Most attempts made with other tools result in the air bubbles reappearing later in the rolling.

How hard should the clay be before I cut my slabs?

Straight-sided work

When making straight-sided work, your slabs need to be stiff enough to retain their shape when picked up. You can use soft clay and cut your slabs in two stages, or complete the cutting in one operation using firm clay.

1. Using soft clay and a template, cut out your slabs slightly larger than necessary. An advantage of this method is that you can knead waste pieces of clay together and reuse immediately.

2. When your slabs have stiffened, cut them to their exact size. Use a ruler edged up to the template to cut against. If you leave your rolled-out clay to stiffen, you can cut your slabs to an exact measurement in one operation. This is obviously quicker, but any leftover clay must be soaked down before reuse.

Soft slabbing work

Clay can be rolled out, cut, and used immediately for soft slabbing work. You may even need to spray your slabs lightly with water and cover them in plastic to keep them damp enough to manipulate. One of the attractions of using this method of construction is that the soft clay will crease, form into folds, and take on stretch marks as shapes are formed. This gives a spontaneous and lively quality to the work, completely different to that of slabbing with hard clay.

The clay seems to pull out of shape while I am cutting slabs, so that I end up with irregular corners. How can I get a more precise result?

Avoiding drag

Using the right tool and technique will stop the clay dragging out of shape at the corners. Cut slabs with a very sharp knife, so that the clay is sliced cleanly. Choose a thin, straight blade that allows you to cut accurately. A knife that slants from edge to edge or from tip to base may cut at a sloping angle, upsetting exact measurements.

1. Stand directly above your work, as this will help you to cut straight down. Move either the slabs or your own position after each cut, so that all of the sides are cut with the same motion and from the same angle.

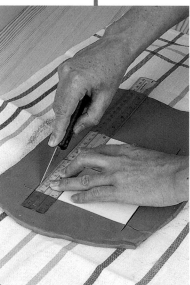

2. To achieve precise corners, start the cut slightly beyond the corner and cut toward the middle. Do this from both corners, so that each side is cut in two movements that meet in the middle.

How do I know what size to make my slabs?

Approximate measuring

You may need only a rough indication of the size of your finished pot. Suppose, for example, that you want to make a pot about 6in (15cm) high, which is tall rather than wide.

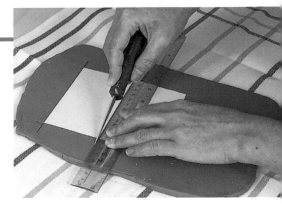

1. Draw a rectangle on your clay, about 6in (15cm) in length, using a ruler and triangle to help you.

2. Cut out your rectangle and use it as a template to make three more rectangles. Join the four rectangles to form the sides of your pot.

3. Place your pot on a rolled-out piece of clay, and cut around the sides to make a base.

Precise measuring

If you want your pot to have more precise dimensions, you must plan your measurements before cutting any slabs. Remember to consider the thickness of clay, and the way you will join your slabs together. First, draw the measurements on paper, and cut out templates from cardboard. Use the templates to cut your slabs to the exact size. Work on clay that is as hard as possible, without being too dry to join, so that the slabs keep their shape when you join them.

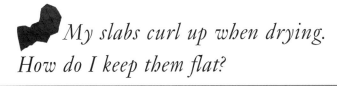 ## My slabs curl up when drying. How do I keep them flat?

Methods to keep clay flat

Curling can be due to uneven drying or to the texture of the clay. Slabs curl if moisture is drawn off one side more quickly than the other, so turning the slabs over several times during drying allows even drying on both sides. Another reason for slabs curling is if you are using a very smooth and dense clay, as this type of clay tends to warp more than an open body. Add sand, molochite, or grog to your clay to open up the texture. Lastly, try using weights. Place some pebbles around the edges of your slabs to weigh them down. This will keep them flat as they are drying.

I make careful measurements for my slab pots, but the last slab never seems to be the right size. How can I make the base fit?

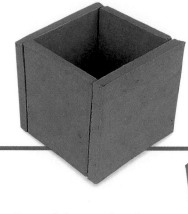

Leave base till last

Do not cut your base until all the sides of your pot are joined. Clay is not a rigid material and the walls of slab-built forms are rarely completely regular. A precisely measured base will not fit because of these irregularities.

1. When you are satisfied with the walls of your pot, place them on a rolled-out piece of clay. Using the walls as a template, cut around them carefully to make your base.

Prop slabs together first

If your measurements are vastly out, you have probably joined the walls of your pot incorrectly. You must make an allowance for the thickness of your clay, and consider how this affects the way you join your slabs. It is easier to understand how the walls of your pots should be joined if you prop them together first. The same four slabs can be used to make a cube (above left) or a rectangle (above right), depending on how you fit the walls together.

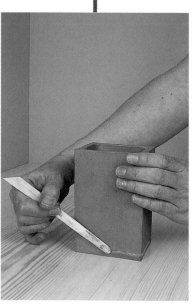

2. Join this base in the usual way with slip or water. A base cut by this method should fit your pot exactly.

How do I roll out slabs which are thinner at one end than the other?

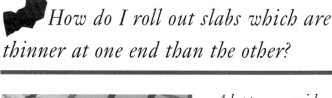

Adapt your guides

Use rolling guides of different thickness. The clay will still be rolled out smoothly, but the thickness will gradually change between the two wooden guides.

How do I stop the seams of my slab-built pot from cracking open?

Join leather-hard slabs

Join the slabs before the clay is too dry. The walls should be leather-hard. Once the clay loses its damp sheen and color, it is too dry to make a good join. Dry all of your slabs to the same extent, so that their shrinkage rate is identical. In the photograph below, the slab on the left is too dry; the slab on the right is just right.

Dry pots slowly

Leave your finished pots to dry slowly. If it is impossible to find a cool spot, wrap the pots in plastic for one or two days before drying them in the air as usual. This allows the seams to settle together.

Secure your seams

Join seams with extreme care. When pots are fired, the heat finds any weak areas, so it is worth spending a little extra time making joins as sound as possible.

1. Scratch and slip the areas of your slabs that are to be joined. Push the slabs firmly into contact, sliding them together until you form a strong bond.

2. Smooth the seam over on the outside, working a little clay back and forward across the join with a modeling tool.

3. To seal the join on the inside, smooth the clay together with your finger or a modeling tool. Then apply slip and smooth in a thin coil of clay, again with your finger or a modeling tool. This will strengthen the seam between the slabs.

4. Pay particular attention to joining the corners, as a seam will often start to split open from this point. Work a thin coil of clay around the corner and across the top seam to reinforce this area.

The walls of my slab-built forms sag inward when drying. How can I support them?

Paper supports

Rigid supports, such as wood, will cause cracking as your pot shrinks when drying. Use scrunched up newspaper, which will support walls but also allow for movement in the drying clay.

Clay supports

Totally enclosed forms can be fitted with a network of clay supports that break large internal areas into smaller sections. Remember to pierce a hole into each enclosed area to allow air and steam to escape. Allow extra time for internal as well as external walls to dry before firing.

What kind of lids can I make for my slab pots?

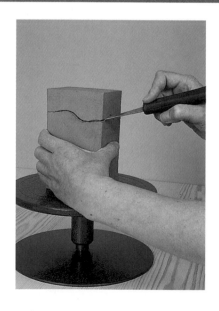

A wavy lid

You can cut a simple but effective lid into a slab pot that has a sealed top and bottom. Try this method on cylindrical and rectangular forms. When the pot is leather-hard, score a wavy line around it, about one quarter down from the top. Cut through the line all the way around the pot, making sure that the two ends meet. The irregularities of the cut line will hold the lid in place. Remove your lid, and neaten the edges of pot and lid. Do not take away too much clay as you smooth the rough edges or your lid will not be a good fit. Put the lid back in place to fire.

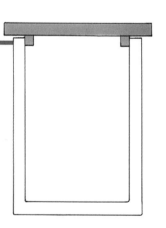 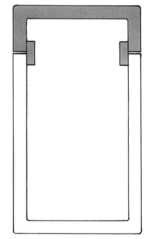

Lids with inner supports

Cut a flat slab to fit on the top of the pot, or a little larger so that it overhangs the walls slightly. Cut two narrow strips of clay and attach them to the underside of the slab, as shown in the diagram on the left. If positioned correctly, the strips will keep the lid in place. You can make a deeper lid by cutting a straight line through a sealed cube. Add strips of clay to the inside of the lid, as shown on the right, so that it sits securely on top of the pot.

I try to sand down my slab-made plinths to make them even, but the sandpaper goes into all the hollows, accentuating the irregularities. What can I do to get a better finish?

Sanding correctly

Rub the plinth onto the sandpaper instead of rubbing the sandpaper onto the plinth. That way, you only sand the raised areas, producing an even side. Place a sheet of sandpaper on a level surface, and rub your plinth over it, making sure that you hold the plinth flat.

Texture your plinth

Instead of trying to make a perfectly straight-sided plinth, exploit the irregularities. Covering your plinth in a texture helps to disguise an uneven shape. Beat your plinth with textured sticks, or push patterned material into the surface. Your plinth will still retain its shape, whether rectangular, square, or cylindrical, but there will be no need to make every side, corner, and curve precise.

Lively shapes

Think about ways of making plinths which are less static.

1. Hit a rectangular plinth with a rolling pin to give it a new shape. Make a hole somewhere first so that air can escape as you reshape the plinth.

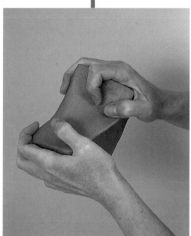

2. Twist a rectangular plinth in your hands while it is still soft. If seams split, you can easily rejoin them to produce a plinth with strong lines of movement running through its form.

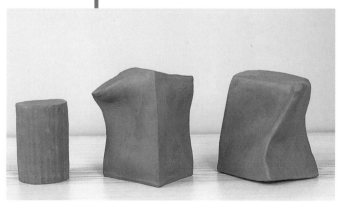

3. A variety of unusually shaped and textured plinths can contribute additional movement and interest to your work. Try cylindrical and irregular shapes as well as squares and rectangles.

What kind of pots can I make from soft slabs of clay?

Cylindrical pots

You can make regular cylindrical shapes, or explore uneven rims and seams as a design feature.

1. Wrap a cylinder, such as a bottle or a cardboard tube, in newspaper. Roll a slab of soft clay around the bottle, keeping one edge of the clay level with the base of the bottle.

2. Cut away the excess clay with a craft knife. Make sure there is enough clay left to create a slight overlap where the two edges meet, so that the join will be secure, but not too much, as this would produce too thick a seam.

3. Smooth the clay around the body of the bottle, making sure there is no air trapped (above). The clay should be soft enough to smooth together easily with either a modeling tool or a finger (right).

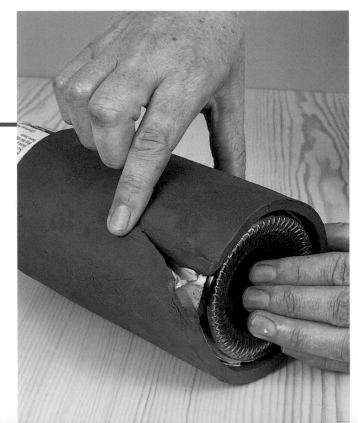

4. Stand your pot on some rolled-out clay and cut around it to form a base. Scratch and slip around the bottom of the tube of clay and attach the cut-out base, smoothing over the seam.

5. When the base is joined, open the paper to release the bottle. You must remove the bottle before the clay has shrunk around it.

6. Now you can smooth and join the seam running down the inside of your pot. Do the same around the inside of the base, using a modeling tool to help you reach the seam.

Slump pot cornucopia

Slump pots need only crumpled paper for support. You can make virtually any shape as long as you provide the right support. The example shown here is a shaped container for hanging plants.

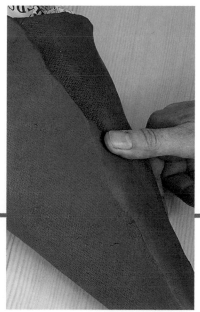

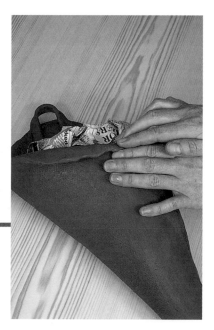

1. Roll a soft slab into a conical shape. Gently hold up one side of the cone, so that the clay does not stick together on the inside.

2. Stuff with crumpled newspaper, to hold the shape of the cone, and join the seam.

3. Finish your cornucopia with a hanging ring and additional shaping or decoration.

I have made many slab pots, and now I would like to find ways of making them look more interesting. What do you suggest?

Discover a new approach

Surface, color, and shape can all provide ideas for varying your work. Look around you for sources of inspiration.

EARLY IMPRESSIONS

Alter the smooth surface of the clay before you begin building your pot. Roll the clay onto texturing material, such as frosted glass, lace, patterned mats, or leaves.

SUBTLE OR BOLD COLOR

Add color to the clay for your pots. Knead it into the clay to give a marbled effect, or use bolder areas of pattern rolled into your clay slabs.

Below: Louis Marak, Hand-held teapot

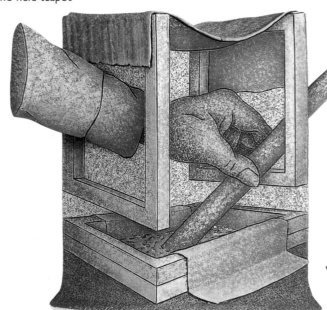

SLAB-BUILT SCULPTURES

Slab building is a quick and strong way of creating an array of shapes. You can develop your work toward sculptural rather than functional pieces, which will open up a wider choice of shapes and decorative effects. Use a combination of straight-sided slabs and soft slabbing to make sculptures based on mechanical or natural forms.

Above: John Blackwell, Slab-built ship

Below: Josie Warshaw, Japanese box

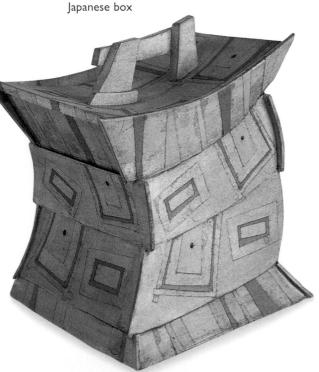

CREATIVE FORMS AND COMBINED TECHNIQUES

Your pots need not be a regular shape. Build pots with unusual angles and changes of direction, and combine techniques to supply interesting additions. Extruded sections work well because of their mechanical nature, and coiled or thrown pieces can make lively extensions. Extruded shapes were used to extend the surface of the teapot shown above, so that the painted picture moves beyond the edge of the pot. In the box to the right, sloping angles and changes of direction are echoed in the decoration.

My tiles go into the kiln flat but come out warped. How can I prevent this?

Rib your tiles

Ribbing one side of the tiles will help to stop them curling. You can do this in several ways. Roll a thin metal bar across the slabs; roll out the slabs on a corrugated plaster bat or mold; or use the edge of a strip of wood to rib a slab of clay. You can then cut the slab into tiles.

Use the right clay

If your tiles are warped, you may be making them with the wrong type of clay. Make tiles with a gritty and open-textured body. The clay does not have to be malleable, so you can include more sand, grog, or molochite than when throwing, pinching, or coiling. Tiles made of paper clay have a good resistance to warping. Another common reason for warped tiles is that they may be too thin. Thick tiles warp less often than thin tiles.

I like decorating tiles but not making them. Are there any shortcuts?

Two shortcuts

Tile cutters are available in a variety of shapes and sizes (below right). Once the clay is rolled out to an even thickness, you can cut the tiles quickly without needing to measure. Alternatively, you can buy bisque tiles which are ready to decorate and glaze (right). The size and choice of clay is limited, but if decoration interests you most, they may meet your needs.

How can I display my decorated tiles in a way that allows me to move and reset them at a later date?

Apply a layer of silicon bathroom sealant to the back of your tiles and stick them to a wooden board. The base must be porous, so use wood or composition board (MDF) that has not been painted or sealed. Lightweight tiles can be attached to a backing with Velcro. Stick pads of Velcro to the back of your tiles, and hook them in place on a board covered with suitable material.

What techniques can I use to make figurative sculptures that are hollow to fire in the kiln?

Hollow out solid figures

You may prefer to make your figures in solid clay, so that you can build and model your sculpture more freely. However, very thick lumps of clay cannot be fired without risking the work splitting or blowing up, so you will need to hollow out such figures before putting them in the kiln to fire.

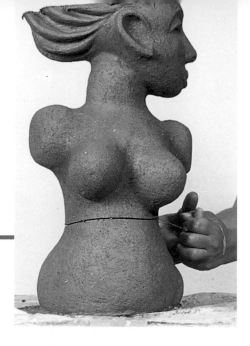

2. Allow the clay to dry out slightly, then cut open the figure with a wire or long-bladed knife. Remove clay from the inside of each piece with a loop tool.

3. Join the seams securely to reform the shape of your figure. It will now be hollow and suitable for firing.

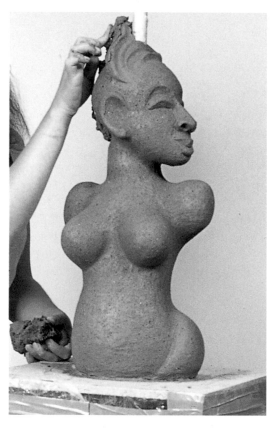

1. Carve your sculpture from one solid block of clay, or build up the piece by joining lumps of clay together. Position a metal or wooden pole inside the clay as an armature if this is necessary to support the weight. Cover the pole in polythene or paper to prevent it sticking to the clay, and remove it when the sculpture is cut open for hollowing.

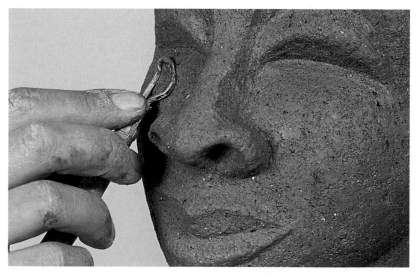

4. Model the fine detail to complete your figure, and make sure there are holes so that the air inside can escape. A large sculpture will need to be left to dry for several weeks before it can be fired.

Using molds

Make molds from a figure modeled in solid clay, then use your press molds to make hollow figures. This is an ideal method, as the molds are reusable.

1. Model a solid figure in clay. A figure that is standing straight with all limbs separate is ideal. Carefully cut your figure into separate arms, legs, hands, feet, torso, and head.

2. Make a simple two-piece mold in plaster of each piece of the figure.

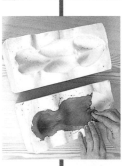

3. Once your molds are dry, press clay into them to make hollow shapes. Join the two halves of each section together so that you have all the separate parts of your figure.

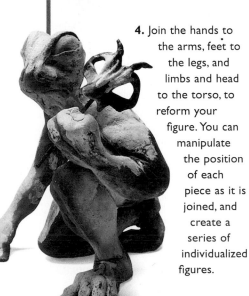

4. Join the hands to the arms, feet to the legs, and limbs and head to the torso, to reform your figure. You can manipulate the position of each piece as it is joined, and create a series of individualized figures.

Building hollow forms

Figures can be built using techniques which give them a hollow form.

COILING

You can coil hollow shapes as the base for figurative work. Strong robust shapes and simple stylized forms are well suited to this technique.

SLABBING

Make your figures from soft slabs. Use soft cylinders and clay slumped over supports to create freely modeled forms. The characteristics of folding and stretching clay helps give a lively quality to this type of work, and you can texture and pattern your clay slabs before you start building, as in the example shown here.

Right: Jan Beeny, Slab-built sheep

THROWING

Use thrown shapes as the starting point for animal and human sculptures. Throwing is a quick way of producing many hollow forms, which you can then manipulate. Experiment with joining shapes together, cutting and reforming shapes, or combine this technique with slabbing and coiling, as in this example.

Left: Gill Bliss, Frogman   **Above:** Janet Hamer, A gaggle of geese

My figures either blow up in the kiln, or chunks of clay split off. How do I stop this from happening?

Make airholes

Hollow forms must have at least one airhole to allow steam to escape. As you pack work into the kiln for firing, check that the holes have not sealed themselves over. You can conceal holes within features such as the nose or mouth, or pierce a vent in the base where it will not show. Use a spike, hole cutter, or drill bit. A hole made by a knife may turn into a split.

Prick the surface

Make sure you allow enough time for your figures to dry. Any damp clay can split or explode during firing. Use a body that contains some sand or grog. When modeling in very smooth, fine clay, it is easy to trap air pockets. Prick the figure all over with a needle. Creating small holes releases any air trapped just below the surface which may cause the clay to flake.

How do I hollow out my work without pushing the clay out of shape?

Hollow out when the clay is leather-hard and firm enough to hold its shape. The inside clay remains softer for longer, so that it is easy to scrape out. Support the outside of the work in your hands or on foam, not on a table or board, which will flatten it. Hollow your figure when the structure is complete, but leave the finer details of your modeling until the figure is reassembled.

How can I stop the seams of my hollow figures opening up during firing?

Keep the clay damp

It is important that the clay does not become too hard to make a successful join. Wrap the cut pieces in polythene while they are waiting to be worked on, and spray with water if they dry out too quickly.

Assess your materials

The cut edges of your figures will wet down more effectively in a more open body, so add grog or molochite to your clay. Adding vinegar to the slip you are using to join pieces together will also help.

Choosing where to cut

Cut your figure where the seams will be under as little pressure as possible. A bent leg, for example, is better cut below or above the knee, not right at the bend. Choosing the position of your divisions carefully will ensure that it is the solid walls of clay and not the cuts that carry most of the weight of the figure. Once the seams have been rejoined, dry your work slowly to minimize the risk of cracking.

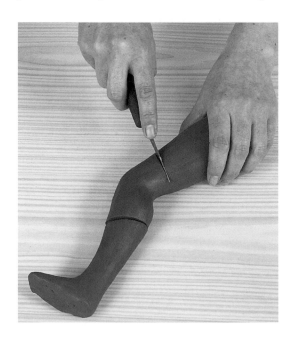

I find it difficult to fit the hollow pieces of my figures together. How can I stop making the edges so thin?

Give yourself a guideline
After cutting your work in half, draw a guideline to establish the thickness of your walls.

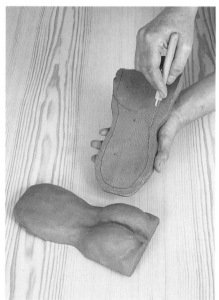

I. Score a line with a knife or needle around the edge of each piece of your figure, leaving sufficient margin for the walls. Stay within the line as you hollow out, and your edges will remain thick enough to join successfully.

2. The easiest and surest way to make sure you stay within the guidelines is to hollow out your figure by working from the edges inward. This way, you will not cross the line by mistake.

The figures I model have legs that are too thick, in order that they can carry the weight of the body. How can I rectify this?

When making a figure whole, the lower legs can slump due to the pressure of weight and the constant small movements that the legs undergo when you are working on the upper body and head. Try modeling the upper body and lower body of your figure separately, completing as much detail as possible so that little or no work needs to be done high up on the figure after the parts are joined. Paper clay is ideal for this type of modeling as you can join wet clay to dry clay. Model the legs of your figure to the appropriate thickness and let them dry. When the clay is absolutely solid, model the upper body. The legs will then be strong enough to take the weight of the additional work. Another option is to include a support as part of the design, something for your figure to stand alongside or hold onto, so that the legs do not have to take all the weight.

How do I support my figures during making, when the clay is wet?

Inside and outside supports
Support figures from the inside using metal rods, wooden sticks, knitting needles, or umbrella spikes as an armature. Leave one end of the armature sticking out of the clay so that you can remove it when the clay is firm, or remove the armature when you hollow out the figure. Support figures from the outside with scaffolding constructed from rods that reach into the model. Remove the rods and heal the holes when the clay is firmer, and put clay props in place for additional support.

How should I support my figures in the kiln so that they do not slump during firing?

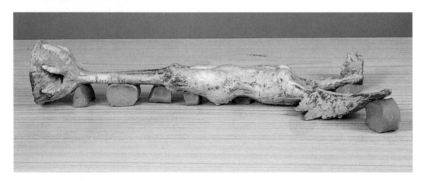

Make clay props

Clay softens while being fired, and parts that are liable to sag need to be propped up with blocks of clay. These should be hollow, but very solid in construction. Make clay props at the same time as the figure, so that the shrinkage rates are the same. It is easy to prop work during a bisque firing, but if you intend to glaze the piece, you must give more careful thought to the position of props so that they do not touch the glaze.

Lay the figure down during firing

It may be easier to prop unglazed figures if they are lying down. Be careful to use suitably shaped props, so that that the figure does not sag out of shape and become flattened to the kiln shelf. Alternatively, push the figure into a thick layer of silica sand. The sand will mold itself around the form of the figure and will not move during firing. It is not possible to use these methods on glazed figures.

My porcelain figures are spoiled by small splits in the fired clay. How can I prevent this?

Porcelain is prone to cracking on thick areas, so thin the walls of your work as much as possible. Try to make the thickness of the walls even as stresses produced by different shrinkage rates within one piece can cause these splits. Dry and fire your work slowly. Even with all these precautions, you will find that the loss rate of imperfect pieces is higher with porcelain than with coarser clays.

Can I leave metal, wood, or wire supports inside the clay during drying and firing?

As a general rule, rigid supports should not be left inside clay. In most cases the clay cracks and shrinks away from the supports while drying and firing. It would only be possible to leave rigid supports in the work if the clay had a very small shrinkage rate – if the clay had additives such as cement or talc, and the firing temperature was low, for example. Metal fired in the kiln can melt, and wood produces noxious fumes. Any experiments using these materials in conjunction with clay must be fired under controlled conditions.

I prop my sculptures, but the supports are never in place after the firing. How can I make them more secure?

Use a clay slab

All the pieces of your sculptures are shrinking around the middle point of the area where they touch the shelf. This causes pieces to move away from one another. To solve the problem, place your work, including the props, on a slab of clay. Remember to use the same clay for your props as for your sculptures, so that the rate of shrinkage is the same.

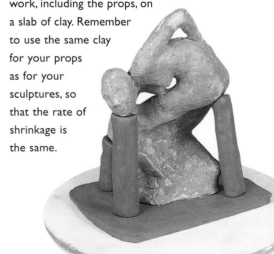

I make each piece of my model separately and join them with slip, but when fired, some part always cracks or splits. What can I do?

Fire separately

Fire your individual pieces separately, and then join them. Using this technique, you can create complex models without needing to worry about warping, splitting, and collapsing. This also makes it possible to give each section its own color or texture, as in the example shown on the right. Think also about making the separate pieces in different materials, such as glass, cloth, or metal, which produces a wider range of textural effects.

Above: Laurance Simon,
La vie en rose

When I cut large sculptures into sections for firing, they warp. How can I prevent this?

Techniques to prevent warping

Make the sculptures in a heavily grogged and open body, and stand the sections on a thin slab of clay or placing sand for firing. This will allow the clay to move easily as it shrinks and not stick to the kiln shelf. Build support walls inside the form, and make sure these line up from one section to the next. In this way any slight movement in the walls should match. Join a coil to the cut edge of each section, to make sturdy rims that will resist warping.

What can I use to join fired sections of sculptures together and sculptures to plinths?

To join small pieces, use an epoxy resin adhesive. Any excess looks like shiny glaze, or can be sanded when hard to give a smooth, matte surface. Car body filler is useful for joining larger sections and adhering sculptures to plinths, because it hardens quickly and can be modeled to become part of the form.

What factors do I need to consider when making large sculptures in several sections?

Careful planning

Designs for such sculptures need to be carefully planned so that they have an overall integrity when finished. Keep checking that the proportions for each piece are right, paying special attention to the areas where it is possible to join them. Large sculptures can also be cut into sections, breaking into the form. You can cut the sections so that the eventual joins cause as little disruption as possible, or accentuate the joins to become part of the form, as in this example.

Right: Christine Derry, Cloak

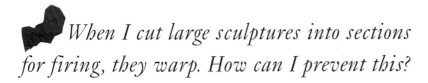

Is it possible to re-fire pieces that have already been joined with glue or body filler? I am frightened they will explode in the kiln.

The filler or glue will simply burn in the kiln, leaving powder instead of solid material. This can be scraped away to allow you to reposition the work before re-gluing. It is important that you check that any airholes have not been sealed over, and that you support pieces that may fall away as the glue disintegrates.

I would like to make some press-molded bowls but do not have any plaster molds. What can I use instead?

Adapting regular dishes
Use ordinary glass, china, or plastic dishes to serve as your molds. Cover them in cling wrap or tissue paper so that the clay does not stick. Since these molds are not porous, the clay will take longer to become firm enough to remove.

Clay molds
Bisque-fired bowls make good molds, because they are porous and release the clay readily. Use them in the same way as plaster molds.

How do I cut a clean rim around press-molded dishes?

Cutting with a knife
When using a knife, turn the mold as you proceed, so that you repeat the same movement from the same angle. Keep the knife flat against the mold and cut away from you as if cutting pastry from the edge of a pie.

Using a wire
Use a harp or taut wire to cut straight across the mold. The clay must be soft to respond successfully.

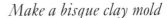

What is the easiest way to make a simple mold of a found object?

Plaster mold

Making plaster molds of found objects can give you a wealth of interesting shapes, textures, and decorative details, which you can repeat exactly as many times as you want.

1. Fill any undercuts or areas of the object which may be difficult to release with clay. Push your object onto a flat slab of clay so that the surface to be molded is facing upward, and coat it with a releasing agent.

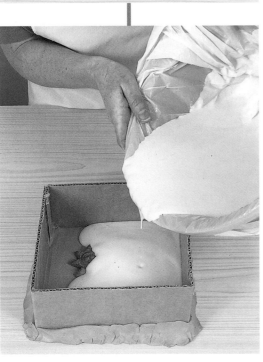

2. Build a wall around the object using clay, cardboard, plastic, or wood. Tie string around the walls to make them more secure, and press thick coils of clay around the outside to brace them further. Mix enough plaster to cover the object and pour it into the space. Remove the walls, clay coils, and object when the plaster has set to reveal your mold.

Make a bisque clay mold

You can reproduce very fine detail by pushing an object into clay. In this way you do not have to worry about undercuts, which would stop the object being released from a plaster mold.

1. Roll out a thick slab of smooth clay, and push your object into the clay, up to its widest point. Roll the object into the clay if this helps to create a good impression.

2. When dry, bisque fire your mold, and use it to produce a low-relief pressing of your object. The bisque mold will give a slightly smaller pressing than the original object because the clay has shrunk in the firing.

I tried to make a simple press mold, but the object stuck to the plaster. How do I stop this happening next time?

Coat your object in a releasing agent to prevent it from sticking to the plaster. You can use talc, cooking oil, vaseline, or soft soap, depending upon the nature of the material. Make sure that you do not lose any fine detailing or texture on your object because of a thick buildup of releasing agent; a very thin layer will suffice.

When making a two-piece mold, how do I know where to make the join line?

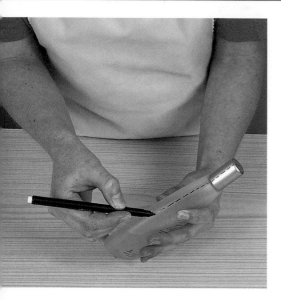

Find the ridge

The join line between two parts of a mold should come at the widest part of the object. It is like the highest point of a ridge in the landscape, and the walls of the object must fall away on both sides. Look straight down on top of your object and find the widest part all the way around. Draw a guideline on your object if this helps you. Bury it in sand or clay up to this line to form the boundary between the two pieces of your mold.

I am making a two-piece mold. How do I make sure that it fits back together in the right place when in use?

Make natches in the mold

To ensure that the mold will fit back together in the right place, you need to make natches in the adjoining surfaces. Before the first half of your mold is fully hardened, make three gently sloping holes in its surface. When you pour the second half of the mold, the plaster will run into the holes in the first half, making small lumps in its surface. You can then use these as a guide to position the mold correctly. You can also buy plastic natches from clay suppliers. Insert three into the surface of the first half of your mold; they will create matching holes in the second half.

What should I use to stop the plaster sticking together when making the second half of a mold?

Several layers of soft soap rubbed into the surface of your mold will give a slippery, impervious surface for the next layer of plaster to sit on. Alternatively, cover the first half of your mold in a thin layer of slip. This will flake away as dry clay when the mold is finished, enabling the two pieces to separate.

How can I stop clay from sticking in my press molds?

Sprinkle with talc

Molds that are fully dry release the clay smoothly. Tap the mold gently on a table to encourage the clay to move. Molds which are a little damp can be given a fine dusting of talc to prevent the clay from sticking. Sprinkle a little talc into the mold and spread it over all areas. Pay particular attention to corners and changes of direction.

I have some simple press molds for dishes and bowls. How can I make the pots from them more interesting?

Make a bottle or vase

Use a dish mold to make the twin sides of a bottle or vase. You can then finish your pot using other techniques, such as throwing, coiling, extruding, or pinching.

1. Push clay into a dish mold to make one half of a bottle or vase. Use small pieces of clay, tightly packed, and then smooth them together with your fingertips, or roll out a complete slab of clay.

2. Release the first half of the pot from the mold, then make the remaining half. When finished, join the two sides together to form the body of your pot.

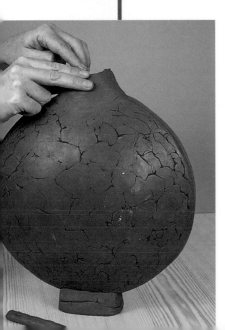

3. Make a footring and cut a hole at the top for the opening. Form the neck by coiling or throwing. Experiment with a variety of differently shaped molds, such as flat dishes and round bowls, to give you a range of interesting vase and bottle shapes.

Colored pots

Press different colored clays into your mold to make interesting and intricate patterns.

1. Lay small pieces of colored clay in your mold to form patterns.

2. Smooth the inside to blend the separate pieces of clay well. The interior of your pot will have very mixed coloring, but the precisely laid out pattern will still be present on the outside.

3. Leave your pot until leather-hard. Scrape both sides with a metal kidney to reveal a more precise pattern of colors.

Texture and pattern

Roll your clay on a textured or colored surface before draping it into the mold. Let the clay form natural folds in the mold to obtain a lively, organic shape. You can also texture the mold itself by cutting into the plaster to make a pattern that will transfer onto your dish.

THROWING SOFT CLAY as it spins on the wheel can be a joy, but it does require patience and practice. Once a degree of proficiency is attained, you can create tableware items such as mugs and teapots, each of which brings new areas of discovery – how to make handles and spouts, for example. Although we generally associate throwing with functional items, it is also an efficient way to produce sculptural work.

Throwing

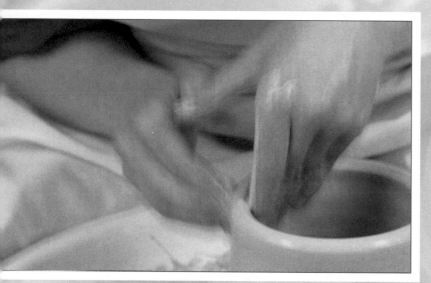

I am learning to throw. Can you suggest some useful tools to buy?

A basic toolkit

Equip yourself with a few personal tools which you know will always be available and in good condition: a bowl that fits inside the wheel tray for holding water; sponges of different sizes to use while you are throwing and for cleaning the wheel; a wire for cutting pots from the wheelhead; and some boards, tiles, or shelves for standing freshly thrown pots to dry. Several old towels, washed for each session on the wheel, are invaluable.

As you progress with your throwing, add some tools that help to refine your pots. Include a tool for trimming the base of a pot before cutting through with a wire; a needle for cutting irregular rims and pricking air bubbles; and ribs to shape and decorate your pots. You can expand this basic toolkit gradually as you widen the scope of your throwing, and find a need for tools to perform specific tasks, such as turning, shaping, and decorating.

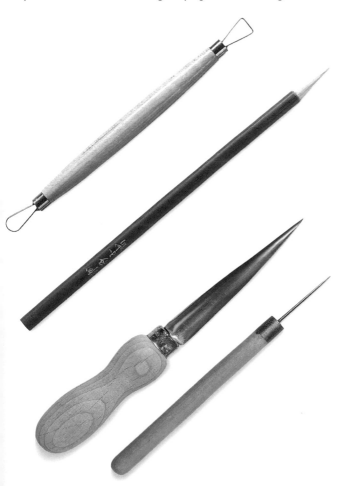

When I throw the clay on the wheel, it flies off again almost immediately. Where am I going wrong?

Slam the clay down

Many beginners try to throw the clay onto the wheel while it is spinning. You cannot attach the clay securely in this way. Slam the clay onto a still wheelhead, keeping hold of the clay all the way down, and it will be pushed firmly into place.

Dry your wheelhead

Water on a metal wheelhead stops the clay adhering properly and must be removed between throwing pots. If throwing on wooden or plaster bats, you may need to dampen the surface slightly for the clay to stick well. Excessive water, however, should always be removed.

I am learning to throw, but find the clay difficult to shape. Why is this?

Many beginners are given clay which is too hard or too soft to use, making throwing a frustrating and exhausting business. Clay that is too soft collapses quickly, and clay that is too hard does not respond to your centering and throwing movements. Try to make sure that your clay is soft, but not sticky. You will soon learn to judge the right consistency, and find that this is a key factor in improving your skills and enjoyment.

I very often trap air between the wheel and the clay. How can I stop this happening?

Make an egg shape

It is not how you put the clay on the wheel, but the shape of the clay that is the problem. Form the clay into a pointed egg rather than a round ball. The point of the egg hits the wheel first and spreads out, so that there is less chance for an air pocket to form.

How can I stop the clay coming off the wheelhead when I grab hold of it?

Use plenty of water

Both your hands and the clay need to be kept wet during throwing. Any dryness causes the clay to stick to your hands and be pulled off the wheel. Place a bowl of water in the wheel tray and dip your hands into this frequently while you are throwing. Use a sponge to trickle water over the clay. During the course of a throwing session, the water in your bowl mixes with clay to make a slip. Many potters prefer to throw with this, since it is well lubricated and less liable to saturate the clay than water.

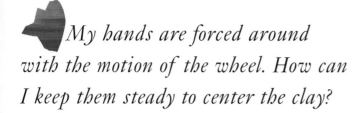

My hands are forced around with the motion of the wheel. How can I keep them steady to center the clay?

Keep your hands moving
You must think about the action of your hands, and not about the action of the wheel. Your hands need to make a squeezing in or pushing down motion to center the clay. Do not let them sit still on the clay, because that makes it harder to stop them following the motion of the wheel.

Supporting actions
Try to support your hands and arms wherever possible. This helps you to maintain a steady throwing posture which is not unduly affected by the motion of the wheel. Tuck your elbows against your body and rest your arms on the side of the wheel tray to give you added strength during throwing. Keep your hands in contact with each other through various positions of your fingers. These movements are very individual and each thrower learns their own preferred methods of support.

How can I keep my fingers in place when the clay is going around?

Smooth your clay
Turn the wheelhead very slowly, and pat the clay to get rid of lumps and irregularities which will knock your hands away. Make your clay as smooth and as close to the center of the wheel as possible. This gives a good start to your centering.

Is it really necessary to spend so much time learning to center the clay?

Learn to center properly
Unless you learn how to center the clay, you will always make wobbly, lopsided pots. When you are new to throwing, time spent centering is essential, and it will prove invaluable when you begin making finished pots. Once you have mastered the technique, centering can be achieved in a few seconds, with very little effort.

I do not seem to have the strength to center the clay. Why am I finding it so difficult?

Practice your technique

Centering is achieved through a well-learned technique. It is practice and not brute strength that will improve your centering. Use a fast wheel speed and clay that is soft enough to raise and lower easily. Both of these factors help to lessen the effort needed for centering.

1. Squeeze the clay inward to make it rise up into a cone. Follow the upward movement of the clay with your hands, continuing the pressure as you work.

2. Change your hand position to push down on top of the clay. Support the clay with the other hand as it falls. Try to move the clay up and down in a continuous motion.

How many times should I move the clay up and down when centering?

If you spend a great deal of time centering, the clay becomes tired and saturated, causing pots to collapse quickly during throwing. An experienced thrower usually needs no more than three up-and-down movements to center the clay. It is only through practice that you will gain this rhythm, and your success rate will improve if you persevere.

Is there an easy way to figure out when my clay is properly centered?

Use a tool

Hold a needle or pointed tool close to the turning clay. Any uneven areas will touch the tool, leaving a mark on the clay. Re-center the clay and repeat this process until no irregularities are found. As your experience grows, you will be able to dispense with the tool and recognize when the clay is running true by the look and feel of the clay.

When I try to center the clay, a well forms in the middle. Sometimes this seals over to form a hole full of water. How can I prevent this?

I can now center the clay successfully, but seem to knock it off-center again during throwing. How can I stop this happening?

Form a dome

Always make the center of the clay the highest point. If you leave the clay flat or with a slight depression, it will sink in the next movement and form a well.

1. Finish your squeezing-up movements by shaping the top of the clay to a point, using the side of one hand as a guide. Take care that you do not raise the clay by pulling up its outside edge. This causes the clay to fold in on itself and sink in the middle. You must squeeze the clay inward, which forces it to rise up from the central point.

2. When you push down again, keep the clay in a domed shape. The center of the clay should remain the highest point. Do not force the middle into a concave shape as you push the clay down.

Throw beyond your pot

Picture to yourself that the walls of your pot are taller than they really are, and keep your hands in their throwing position until you reach the imaginary height of your pot. Continuing to throw beyond your pot in this way prevents you from making any sudden, jarring movements as you reach the true rim of your pot.

Examine your centering

You may only be centering the outside of your clay. Check that you are moving all of the clay up and down during centering, and not just smoothing the outside.

I have difficulty centering a large weight of clay. Do I need to change my technique?

Divide the clay

It is possible to center a large amount of clay by dividing it and working on each portion separately.

1. Cut the large weight of clay into pieces of a more manageable size. Center one of the sections of clay in the usual way. Dry the top of the clay so that the second section will stick firmly.

2. Attach a second portion of clay to your centered piece, and work to center this portion in turn. You can combine the two centered weights of clay for throwing, or continue to add more clay in the same way.

Correct stance

Centering large amounts of clay may require a different throwing posture. Find ways of standing or pushing from your legs, which enables you to use the entire weight of your body and not just your arms and hands.

Wooden ribs

If your fingers buckle when you try to center large lumps of clay, you may find it helpful to hold a rib or piece of wood against the clay. Sometimes it is possible to exert more concentrated pressure when using such a tool.

When I push down with my thumb to make a hole in the clay, I push the clay off-center. How can I make the hole straight?

Support your hands

Your hands need to be held firmly, so that they push straight down and do not wander off-center. By making the hole with both thumbs, you can push together as well as down. This gives your thumbs the support they need to remain straight. If you only use one thumb, rest that hand against your other hand. You then form a support that keeps your working thumb steady.

My thumb gets stuck in the hole I make in the clay. How can I release it without knocking my pot off-center?

Use plenty of water to lubricate your thumb as you push it into the clay, which is very dry inside. As you reach the bottom of the hole, press your thumb outward to widen the opening and start forming the base of your pot. As you become more experienced, you will be able to open the hole and widen the base in one flowing movement.

I have made the hole in my lump of clay. What should I do to widen it ?

Cylinders
You must be clear at this stage whether you are making a cylinder or bowl form, because each requires different movements. To make a cylinder, push your thumb outward straight across the wheelhead, to form a flat base. You can then pull up the walls of your pot in subsequent movements.

Bowls
Begin to form the inside of a bowl from the very first widening movements. Push your thumb in an upward curve to open out the clay. Support the walls of your bowl with a hand on the outside of the clay.

Whenever I try to make a pot on the wheel, it collapses. What am I doing wrong?

Use fewer moves
Sometimes pots collapse because the clay is saturated with water and overworked. You need to complete your pots in fewer moves, both during centering and throwing. As you are throwing, sponge out any excess water in the center of your pot, and only wet the clay when necessary.

Weak areas
A pot may collapse due to a weakness, such as an air bubble, a soft lump of clay, or an excessively thin area. Make sure you prepare your clay thoroughly, and avoid thinning the walls of your pot unduly. Cutting a failed pot in half will often let you see any unevenness in your throwing.

Many of my pots have holes in the bottom when I cut them off the wheel. How can I judge the thickness of the base?

Use a needle

Stop pushing your thumb down when you know there is still plenty of clay left, and test the depth of the base with a needle.

1. Stick a needle straight down into the center of your pot. Mark on the needle where the tip disappears into the clay. Any holes made in this way will quickly seal over.

2. Pull the needle out of your pot to reveal the thickness of the clay. Repeat this process after adjusting the thickness of the clay until you achieve the thickness of base you need.

My cylinders have humps in the base. What can I do to correct this?

Keep thumbs straight

When you widen the base of your pot, make sure that your thumb moves straight across and does not push farther down into the clay. During throwing, take care to leave the base untouched.

Smooth it out

Correct an existing hump by working backward and forward across the clay with your thumb, fingers, or a sponge. Do this before any throwing of the walls, because it will be much harder to smooth out at a later stage.

Many of my pots crack across the base while drying. What can I do to prevent this?

Saturated bases

Bases of drying pots can crack when the clay is much wetter in this area than the walls. Sponge out the water that collects at frequent intervals during throwing, and never leave water in a finished pot. Turning your pots over to dry, once the rims are strong enough to take the weight without distorting, can help to dry your pots more evenly.

Uneven thickness of clay

Pots that have very thick or very thin bases may crack because of the stresses of uneven drying rates. Try to correct this in your throwing, and turn or scrape away very thick bases if necessary.

When I try to throw a cylinder, it gets wider and wider and I end up throwing a bowl. What must I do to keep the sides straight?

Shape walls inward

Keep the shape of your pot curving inward during throwing. It is simpler to adjust an inward curve in the final shaping than a wall that has flared outward. Throw with your outside fingers slightly higher than your inside fingers, so that the clay is squeezed slightly inward as well as upward. Continue in this way until the final shaping of your pot, when you can straighten the walls.

Collaring

Slow the wheel when throwing cylinders. The faster the wheel, the more centrifugal force pushes the walls out. It is easier to control the clay at a slower speed. Hold your hands around your pot and move from the base to the rim, squeezing in as you progress upward. Use a collaring action in between pulling up the clay to help control the shaping.

How do I stop the rim of my pot from buckling into folds?

A pot usually folds at the rim when the clay is thin, oversaturated, or tired. Make sure you are moving the thickness of clay from the bottom of the walls completely through to the rim. This prevents the top of your pot from becoming overworked. You can also leave a thickness of clay at the rim of your pot to give it added strength.

What can I do to neaten uneven rims?

Trim uneven rims

Irregular and badly shaped rims are best removed completely. This gives you a second chance to finish your pot successfully.

1. Using the wheel at high speed, push a needle or sharp knife into the clay below the ragged edge of your pot. Keep your hand very steady. Hold your other hand inside your pot where the needle will meet a finger.

2. As you feel the needle touch your finger, allow the pot to make a complete revolution, then lift both hands decisively, taking the needle and old rim with you.

3. The rest of your pot should be undisturbed, and you can smooth and shape the new rim with a damp sponge to give a better finish.

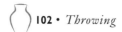

The rims of my pots always look thin and weak. What will improve them?

Strengthen rims

Remember that the thickness of rims shrinks in firing, along with the overall size of your pots. Leave a thickness of clay at the rim of your pot throughout throwing. You can adjust this slightly in your final shaping, but keeping an accentuated rim strengthens the form. Press your finger or a sponge over the top of your pot as you throw. This helps to consolidate the clay and keep the rim firm.

I would like to throw some rounded, high-sided bowls, but they turn into flat dishes. What shaping movements should I be making?

Begin at the base

You must start to form the concave curve of a bowl at the initial stages of opening out. Do not make a flat base and expect to correct it later.

1. Start a bowl before you open out, by forming the clay into a rounded shape. Push your fingers in at the base to make an undercut. Work at a slow speed of the wheel to lessen the effects of centrifugal force.

2. As you open out the clay, form a curve which closes in at the top. It is much easier to widen this shape later than to correct an ever-widening rim.

3. Concentrate on giving the walls height until the clay is thinned sufficiently. As you finish your bowl, let it take up the fullness of its final shape. You can use metal, wooden, or plastic ribs to help give your bowl a smooth inside curve.

The walls of my pots collapse around the base when I cut them off the wheel. How do I stop this?

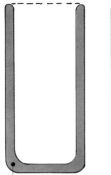

Good thickness at base will support walls

Thin walls at base leave walls unsupported

Strengthen walls

The weight of the walls is carried by the thickness at the bottom. Any undue thinning in the area where the walls join the base causes a structural weakness in the pot, as shown on the right. Make a wide enough base for your pot. If you push the clay out farther just above the base, the walls have no support and buckle. It is better to leave an extra thickness of clay at the base of a pot, which can be turned away when the clay is firmer, but leave enough clay when turning in this area to support the walls, as shown on the left.

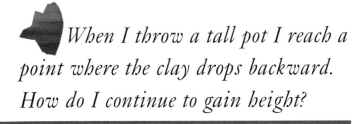

When I throw a tall pot I reach a point where the clay drops backward. How do I continue to gain height?

Improve your throwing

Clay that will no longer gain height may have become saturated and weak. Although the pot has not collapsed, the clay is too wet to take any more thinning. To correct this, begin by pulling tall pots up to their full height in as few moves as possible, and then look more closely at the shaping.

Improve your clay

Change your clay to a body that has greater throwing strength. There are many clays on the market which are formulated for throwing large items. It is more difficult to make a smooth, dense clay gain height. If you wish to continue using the same clay, knead in some sand or grog to open up the texture.

The walls of my bowls and cylinders are always a little lumpy and irregular. Is there anything I can do to throw more smoothly?

Throwing rhythm

Even walls are made by consistent thinning, using regular pressure and a steady upward movement. Practice will give you the necessary throwing rhythm to achieve this.

Use a rib

You can smooth your pot by using a metal, wooden, or plastic rib. Hold the rib against the outside of your pot and push the clay from the inside with your other hand. Squeezing the clay against the rib as you move up the walls produces an even finish.

Turning

As a final resort, uneven walls can be smoothed by turning. It is always better, however, to improve your throwing skills than to rely on correcting mistakes in this way.

Sometimes I find air bubbles in the walls of pots I am throwing. Can I do anything to save these pots?

Prick with a pin

Pricking the air bubble with a pin often releases the air without disrupting your pot, and you can carry on throwing. The clay may heal itself over, but sometimes a weak spot is formed. In these cases, it is better to start again with a ball of clay that was prepared more thoroughly. If you are able to finish throwing a pot and leave the air bubble intact, it is possible to get rid of the air when the clay has hardened a little. At this stage you are less likely to distort the shape of your pot. Prick the air bubble with a pin to release the air and smooth the clay. This area may remain a weak spot in your pot, unless you are able to repair the wall effectively.

Is any preparation necessary before cutting my pots off the wheel?

Clear excess water

Use a sponge to soak up any water left inside your pot. Hold a sponge or rib against the outside to clear away excess water or slip. Taking a little time to clean your pot as much as possible allows you to move it more easily.

Make an undercut

Use an angled tool to make an undercut at the base of your pot. This neatens the base, and helps the wire to cut cleanly through the clay.

The bases of my pots are uneven when I cut them from the wheel. What should I do?

When you cut through your pot, keep the wire taut and flat against the wheelhead. Any buckle in the wire will cut a chunk out of your pot. The wire must have toggles or loops at each end, so that you can hold it firmly. Let the wheel spin slowly as you cut through your pot. Push the wire down onto the wheelhead with your fingers as well as pulling outward from each end of the wire. Bases of large flat bowls and plates are particularly difficult to cut flat. Take care to keep the wire on the wheelhead to the very end of the cut, so that you do not scoop a lump of clay out as the wire is released.

How do I move my pot from the wheel without crushing it in my hands?

Using water

Separate your pot from the wheelhead with a layer of water. This allows your pot to slide from its position and onto a waiting tile.

1. When you finish throwing your pot, pour water onto the wheelhead and drag some of this underneath your pot as you cut through with a wire. Use your wire several times, taking water underneath your pot with each cut.

2. Choose a tile or piece of wood as a platform for your pot. Wet the tile thoroughly, so that your pot can slip across the surface. Push your pot at base level and gently slide it across the wheelhead and onto the waiting platform. If your pot sticks, lubricate it with more water.

Pick up your pot

Newly thrown pots have a certain amount of spring and strength, and can be lifted directly from the wheelhead. Picking pots up in your hands needs a confident and direct approach. It is important to clean excess water or slip from your pot, and to have dry hands. You can use this method to lift cylindrical pots and bowls.

Use a bat

Large or flat pots are always difficult to move from the wheel when the clay is soft. It is easier to throw such pots on a bat, which you can remove from the wheelhead, leaving the pot intact. You can then continue throwing and leave the first pot on the bat until it is firm enough to handle. You can buy bats from clay suppliers or make your own.

1. Place your hands around the body of a cylinder and lift. Rocking your pot from one side to the other helps to release the clay from the wheel. Remember to have a board waiting to receive your pot.

2. Experiment with different hand positions, letting your fingers spread open to provide support at the base of the pot. The key factor in lifting pots is to make strong and steady movements without any hesitation.

I am left with a thin pad of clay when I cut my pot from the wheel. Should I remove it?

An ideal platform

The pad of clay left by the previous pot is an ideal platform on which to start throwing your next pot. Subsequent balls of clay adhere more readily to this than to the metal wheelhead. Clean the pad over with a sponge if it is wet and slippery, but only remove it completely at the end of a throwing session. The pad will be too hard to use after a break from throwing.

The rims of my bowls distort when I lift them off the wheel. Is there any way I can prevent this without having to throw on bats?

Cover with paper

Carefully place a piece of paper on top of your thrown bowl and lightly smooth around the rim with a fingertip, to make a seal between paper and bowl. Now you can cut through your bowl and move it from the wheel without distortion. Air trapped inside the bowl by the paper helps to maintain its shape.

Using heat

Use a hairdryer or a heatgun used for paint stripping to stiffen large or flattened rims. As you aim the heat at your pot, keep the wheel turning slowly, so that all areas of the pot are dried evenly.

Can I introduce color into my thrown pots?

Dynamic lines of color

Introduce color to your pots as you throw them. Begin a pot in the usual way, but stop before the walls are fully extended. Roll out some coils of different-colored clay and push these into the walls of your pot on the inside and outside. Continue to throw, developing the spiraling lines of color as you shape your pot.

Agateware

You can throw with clay that is a mixture of colors. The marbled pots made in this way are known as agateware. Combining the color well produces intricately marbled pots, whereas thicker stratifications of color result from less thorough mixing. Turning these pots when leather-hard reveals a crisper, more intense patterning.

What can I use ribs for when throwing my pots?

Helping to lift

Use ribs to help you move the clay during centering and throwing. They are useful if you find your fingers digging too deeply into the clay. Hold the rib on the outside of the form, and push against it with the fingers of your other hand, inside of the pot. Move up the walls of the pot to raise the clay.

Shaping

Ribs give a sharper definition to the profile of your pots. Use a straight-sided rib on the outside of a cylinder, and a shaped rib to give an exact curve to the inside of a bowl.

How can I get a smooth finish on the rims of my pots?

Sponges with an open texture leave marks on thrown pots. Denser sponge, such as cosmetic sponges or upholstery stuffing, are more satisfactory. Strips of chamois leather, pieces of thin rubber, or polythene, stretched between the fingers, leave a smoother finish. Experiment with different materials to find one that suits your needs.

How can I give a decorative finish to my pots at the throwing stage, so that turning is unnecessary?

Shaped ribs

If your pots are going to be finished at the throwing stage, you could develop some decorative features during their making. Shaped tools or ribs pushed into a pot are useful for giving character to the base and rim.

1. Make a shaped rib by cutting and filing an old credit card, or a piece of plastic or wood. You can quickly produce a range of designs of different shapes and sizes.

2. Hold a shaped rib against the clay, supporting the inside with your other hand. Your thrown pots will have a distinct, ornamental finish without the need for turning.

I find it difficult to flatten out the clay for throwing plates. How can I make it easier?

The right clay

You should always throw plates with soft clay. Hard clay will not flatten to the wheelhead properly, causing air to be trapped more readily. As you push down to form your plate, keep the clay wider at the base. Push down with the palm and side of your hand, moving the clay right from the middle to the edge with each push. A rib can help to press out the clay. A convex shape, rather than a straight-sided rib, will give a smooth, flat surface to your plate.

The rims of my plates usually flop. How do I stop this from happening?

Try to use as little water as possible. You need soft clay for throwing plates, but it is important not to oversaturate the clay. Take care when you are forming the rim of your plate not to push your fingers in at the base or undercut too far with a tool. This can cause a weakness in this vital area of support. Cut a plate that has collapsed in half to see if this is your problem.

I want to throw plates with wide rims. What techniques can I use?

Vertical wall

As you flatten the clay across the wheelhead, leave a thickness at the edge to form the rim. Use this thickness to throw a wall, rising gently from the base.

1. Shape and clean up the base of your plate ready for cutting through with the wire. It is easier to do this while the rim is still vertical and your fingers have room to maneuver.

2. Use a rib to flatten the vertical wall and shape the inside of the plate. As the wall is pushed down, it will also extend in width to form a rim for your plate.

Attach a coil

The rim of a large plate can be thrown from a thick coil of clay which has been added to a flat base.

1. Attach a thick coil of soft clay to a thrown base. Carefully work on both sides of the coil to achieve a smooth, strong join.

2. Now you will have plenty of clay to form a large rim to your plate. You can use a rib to help shape the rim if necessary.

What is the best way to attach bats to my wheelhead?

A layer of clay

Bats can be stuck to the wheelhead, using a layer of clay.

1. Throw 1½–2lb (675–900g) of clay flat across the wheelhead as if you were making a plate. Create ridges in the clay to help release the bat when necessary. The layer of clay must not be too thick, or your bats will slide about as you are throwing.

2. If your bats are very dry, sponge them with water to help them stick to the clay. Place your bat on the wheel, and turn the wheel slowly to tap it into place. Give several good thumps with your fist over the surface of the bat, to seal it firmly to the layer of clay underneath.

Stud fittings

Some wheelheads are drilled with holes for screw-in studs. The bats have holes that fit over these studs, securing them to the wheelhead. Ask your wheel or clay supplier to fix studs into your wheelhead if you wish to use this method of holding bats on the wheel. If you do, you must always have a bat on the wheel. It is possible to cut successive pots from this one bat, or to keep changing the bats as you throw your pots.

Lotus wheelhead

The lotus wheelhead is a special system which replaces the normal wheelhead. Pots are thrown on tiles which are contained within a metal ring. Each tile is removed by pushing up through holes in the wheelhead, and then another can be slotted into place for the next pot. This is a very efficient though more expensive system.

How do I turn flat bowls and plates over for drying without damaging the rims?

Make a sandwich

Sandwich your flat bowls and plates between two boards. It is then easy to flip them over for drying without damaging their rims.

1. Place your plate on a flat board, and wait until the rim is firm enough to take weight without distorting. Lay a second board on top to form a sandwich, with your plate in the middle.

2. Flip the entire sandwich over and take the first board away. Your pot will be neatly turned upside-down to dry the base. Flat, wide bases sometimes sink as they dry upside-down, so check your plates and dishes regularly to find any that need pushing back flat, before they dry too hard to rectify.

I would like to throw big pots but find it difficult to cope with a large amount of clay. Are there any special techniques I can use?

Add a coil

You can increase the size of your pots by adding more clay at intervals during throwing. Throw a weight of clay that you find manageable, and leave a thick rim on the pot. Let this rest to firm up a little, then join a thick coil or a thrown collar of clay to the rim. Throw the attached coil to add height to your pot. Add as many coils as you wish to make your pot grow in sections.

Join two pots

You can throw two separate pots, each with a weight of clay that you find manageable, and then join the two pots together to form one large pot.

1. Throw a pot and measure the rim. Keep a good thickness of clay at the rim to help you when joining the next pot.

2. Throw a second cylinder, making the rim the same size as the first. Allow both pots to dry a little.

3. Join the two pots rim-to-rim. Cut the base from the top pot and rework the two to make a fully unified shape.

I have tried to throw goblets all-in-one with little success. Is there an easier way?

Make in two parts
Throw all the stems and cups for your goblets separately and join them when they are leather-hard. Turn a cup, and while it is still upside-down on the wheel, attach a stem. Let the turning of the wheel help you to position the stem straight. Remember to score and slip both cup and stem to make a firm join. A stick is useful for smoothing the joined area on the inside of the stem.

Use a collar of clay
Attach a collar of soft clay to a turned cup, and use this to throw a stem. You can leave such stems as they are thrown, or refine them with turning when they are leather-hard.

I. Throw all the cups for your goblets and leave them until ready for turning. Now throw some small collars from a hump of clay.

2. Turn a goblet cup, and while it is still attached to the wheel, join a thrown collar to the base. The cup will need to be scored and slipped. Once it is firmly attached and smoothed in, throw the collar of soft clay into the stem of your goblet.

When making small items, I find it very awkward to throw with so little clay. Is there an easier way?

Throw from a hump
It is easier to throw small items when your fingers are raised from the wheelhead. Use one large hump of clay to throw several small pots, instead of struggling with individual amounts. When the pot is finished, use a sharp tool to make a division between the pot and the rest of the clay. Cut through with a wire and remove the pot. Continue to throw more pots with the remaining clay.

The eggcups I throw off a hump of clay often split. How do I prevent this?

Small items thrown off a hump have a tendency to split in the base because the clay in this area has not been worked and is therefore not consolidated enough. Turning the bases of these small pots, or at least running a tool several times over the base, helps to alleviate the problem. It is easy to leave too thick a base on pots cut off a hump, and these often crack in drying. Try to assess the depth of clay better, and cut through closer to the thrown work.

Is it possible to make pots on the wheel that are not round?

Reshape round dishes

Round dishes can easily be reshaped into oval forms. Choose a dish that is firm enough to hold its shape on handling, but will manipulate without cracking. Alternatively, if your dish is leather-hard, cut it into sections and rejoin them to form an oval pot.

1. If using a soft pot, cut a leaf-shaped section from the base of your dish. Gently squeeze the walls until the cut edges meet.

Reshape cylinders

Throw a cylinder, and when it is leather-hard, cut out the base. Squeeze the walls into the desired shape. Place the wall on a rolled slab of clay and cut around it to make a new base. You can make many different shapes in this way.

2. Score and slip the seam and seal over with added clay if necessary. Work on the inside and outside of the base to smooth the join.

3. If your dish is leather-hard, turn it upside-down and mark a line across the center. Measure ¾in (2cm) to each side of the center line and cut through the dish along these two lines. Discard the central section. Join the two remaining sections securely to make an oval dish.

Refashion soft clay

Reshape your thrown pots before they are cut from the wheel by pushing the soft clay from the inside or outside. Experiment with forming indentations; squaring the walls; and making spiral movements. Pots that are adapted in this lively way generally need to be finished at the throwing stage, since turning is not usually possible on the new shapes. If you wish to refine your pots with turning first, you can often re-wet leather-hard clay and manipulate the form to some extent.

When I make the thin neck of a bottle or vase, the clay buckles. What can I do to stop this from happening?

Join a collar

You can throw a bottle shape in sections by adding a collar or coil of clay. This puts less strain on the area where the opening of the bottle is reduced in size.

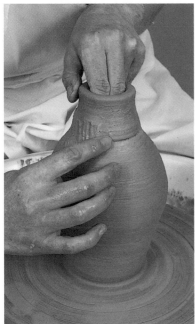

1. Leave the main body of a thrown pot to stiffen a little and throw a small collar of clay. Join the collar to your pot, using a slow wheel to help you center the new clay.

2. Once the added section is securely joined and smoothed in, shape the neck of your bottle.

Fresh clay

Leave a thick area of clay at the top of the pot. This should be fresh and not overworked or saturated with water. When you start to shape the neck, use a faster speed of the wheel and make collaring as well as pulling-up movements with your hands.

How can I see the shapes of my pots accurately during throwing?

When you look at your pots from above, the shape is foreshortened. When throwing, take time to lean over and look at the shape you are forming directly from the side. If you cannot see a clear picture of the profile, get off the wheel and walk around your pot before finishing the shaping. Propping a mirror so that you can see your pot from the side can help.

To make thin-walled porcelain pots, must I throw them thicker than desired and turn down the walls?

It is possible to throw porcelain pots very thinly without walls collapsing if you mix some sugar or syrup with your throwing water. This sticky solution is a good lubricant, and allows you to throw with less water. The clay is less saturated, making finer throwing feasible.

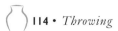

I have tried making lips on my pitchers immediately after throwing, but the entire pot is pulled out of shape. What am I doing wrong?

Saturated clay

The rim of your pot may be so saturated with water that it cannot hold its shape. Try to complete the throwing of your pitcher in fewer moves so that the clay has some strength left. If you think your pot is very wet, let it rest for a while before attempting to shape the lip.

Strong shapes

When throwing a pitcher, make some features that will strengthen the form. Leaving a thickness of clay at the rim; making a change of direction between the body and the neck; and forming a ridge at the top section of the pot, are all ways to help maintain the shape as the lip is being formed.

What kind of lips can I make for my pitchers after turning?

Add a lip

Form the lip of your pitcher by adding a V-shaped section of clay to the thrown body of your pot. Fashion the lip from a rolled-out slab of clay, or cut it from a small thrown bowl. Cut away a section of pot where the new lip is to be joined.

Right: Morgen Hall, Small pitcher with added lip

Cut a lip

Throw a vase form and turn it when leather-hard. Do not make the neck of the vase too flared, because the lip will be pulled out as part of the shaping. Cut a section of the neck away, leaving enough clay standing proud to form a lip. Smooth with a sponge to round the sharp edges of the cut clay. Hold the sides of the remaining clay with one hand and gently pull the middle down to shape the lip. Rub the end of the lip to make a thin edge.

How can I make closely fitting lids for my pots?

Using calipers
Make exact measurements for fitting lids with two sets of calipers.

1. Having thrown the body of your pot, set the inside measurement of the rim on calipers. It is important to use the calipers with the arms crossing over, so that an internal measurement can be recorded accurately.

2. Transfer this measurement to a second set of calipers which are positioned in the opposite way to record external measurements.

3. When you throw the lid for your pot, use the second set of calipers to show you the measurement required.

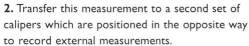

I would like to make some interesting knobs for my thrown pots. What do you suggest?

A variety of knobs
You can throw a knob at the same time as you throw the lid if you are making a lid the right way up. Make sure that the stem is tall enough and the knob large enough for the lid to be picked up easily. With many kinds of lid, you can attach a lump of clay to the leather-hard lid and throw this into a knob. Knobs can also be thrown separately off a hump and attached when both lid and knob are leather-hard (below). Other methods of making knobs include modeling, pressmolding, pulling, twisting, and rolling the clay (below left).

Right:
Nancy Pickard,
Textured knob

Left: Christine McCole,
Lidded jars

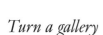

I tried to turn down the rim of a pot to form a gallery, without success. How do I make this sort of lid fitment?

Split a thick rim

To make a pot with a gallery, you must have enough clay at the rim to work with. If you find that your pot is folding in on itself, let the pot rest for a while. You can also try making the gallery before your pot is fully formed, and then completing the shaping.

2. Use a finger or a square-edged tool to split the thickness of the rim and push down one half. This area will form the gallery. Leave behind enough clay to make a substantial rim for your pot so that it does not appear too thin. Work the clay in both the rim and the gallery to perfect the shape.

1. As you throw your pot, leave a thickness of clay at the rim. Push down on the rim of the pot to flatten it toward the middle. You must support the clay from the inside as you make the gallery.

Turn a gallery

A shallow gallery can be turned into a leather-hard pot, provided you leave enough clay at the rim. Throw the pot so that there is extra thickness at the rim. Use a square-shaped turning tool to cut a gallery into the thick area of clay when the pot is leather-hard, then round off sharp edges with a sponge or wetted finger.

Making a teapot seems difficult because of all the different pieces. In what order should I throw and join the separate parts?

The right order

There are two main difficulties in making a teapot: learning to throw separate pieces so that they look complementary when put together, and making sure all the pieces are at the right state of dryness when being joined.

1. Throw the body and lid of your teapot and let these dry until they are leather-hard. Throw the spout at a later time. If you choose to throw the spout at the same time, wrap it in plastic to stop it from drying too much.

2. Turn the body and lid of the pot when leather-hard, if necessary, and cut the spout from its base. Hold the spout up to the pot to see what angle needs to be cut away. Mark where the spout will fit, and make a pattern of holes in this area of the pot, using a hole-cutter or drill bit.

Why are the cut ends of my teapot spouts always crooked?

Twisting spouts

Thrown spouts twist when fired due to a memory that the clay retains of the spiraling action of throwing. If you cut the ends of your spouts, you must allow for this twisting by cutting at an angle. Use a knife or wire and cut the spout diagonally from the bottom right to the top left. The amount of twist in the spout depends on the type and thickness of clay, and the temperature reached in firing. You need to discover the correct angle for cutting by trial and error, according to your particular circumstances.

3. Score and slip both the pot and spout, and join them together. Look straight down onto the top of the pot to make sure the spout is straight. The tip of the spout should be slightly higher than the rim of the pot, so that tea does not pour out before the pot is full.

4. Finish your teapot with a handle, making sure that it is aligned directly opposite the spout. You can put a small hole in the lid of the pot to let steam escape, if you consider this to be a useful feature.

Can I make spouts which do not twist in the kiln?

Molded spouts

You can make a mold of a spout from one that you have modeled, carved, or thrown, or taken from a bought teapot. A two-piece plaster mold is the most serviceable. Press- or slip-molded spouts can be added to thrown bodies successfully and they do not twist during firing. Make different sizes, shapes, and ornamental styles so that you have a choice of spouts.

Using a spout former

Use a spout former to shape rolled-out clay into the desired shape. Spouts made in this way will not twist out of shape during firing. You can make a former in clay, wood, or plaster.

Left: Peter Meanley, Salt-glazed teapot with molded spout

1. Throw or model a range of spout shapes in clay. Hollow out the shapes, and bisque fire them to make formers.

2. Roll out a thin slab of clay and shape this around your spout former. Cut the clay to size and join the seam. Leave the clay to firm a little.

3. Cut open the seam again, and ease the former out of the clay covering. Repair your newly formed spout, and attach it to your teapot in the usual way.

My teapot spouts always crack around the base where they join the pot. What can I do to stop these cracks appearing?

Keep spouts damp

Do not let your spouts dry out too much before attaching them to the pot. Spouts thrown at the same time as the main body of the pot often dry more quickly because they have less clay in them. Keep spouts wrapped in plastic if necessary so that they are still soft enough to give a little as they are shaped around the pot. When you finish making your teapot, wrap it in plastic for a day or two to slow down the drying. This allows all of the parts to settle together before the clay starts to shrink.

Prepare a large area

The area that the clay from the spout reaches as you join it to the pot can be much wider than you may at first anticipate. Scratch and slip the pot well beyond the line made by drawing around the spout.

Add a wet spout

Throw the spout after you have turned the body and lid and made the holes in your teapot. Cut the spout from its base and attach it to the pot immediately. Although the pot is drier than the spout, cracks seldom appear where they join because the soft spout can move and mold itself easily around the pot. Score and slip the body before adding the wet spout to form a good bond.

I would like to learn the skills of repetition throwing. Can you give me any tips?

Throwing rhythm

Repetition work is made in batches, with each stage completed on every pot before moving onto the subsequent stage. Build up a rhythm of throwing so that a few essential movements are repeated for each piece of clay. Stop throwing a lump of clay that has become difficult and start again with a new ball; struggling to adjust misshapen form will prevent you from establishing a flow of movements. The first few pieces you throw at the start of each session will probably not be as well thrown as subsequent pots. Use them as a way of getting into your rhythm and not as a guide for measuring all your work.

Prepare well

It is important that the layout of your work area, the setting out of your tools, and your access to the work does not interfere with your throwing rhythm. Stopping to sharpen tools or look for more clay totally destroys the flow. Good preparation of the clay is vital, so do not skimp time on this.

Keep a logbook

Record all weights of clay, measurements of pots, and so on, which need to be repeated. Do not risk trying to keep them all in your head.

I want to throw a set of mugs. How do I throw them the same size?

Weigh the clay

You must throw each mug with an equal amount of clay. The clay should also be the same consistency for all. After wedging and kneading, cut the clay into 8–12oz (230–340g) balls. Try to develop a good rhythm to your throwing, so that each mug is completed with comparable movements, and you should achieve a suitably matching group.

Measuring sticks and calipers

Mark on a flat stick the height of a pot you want to repeat. Write the name of the pot alongside the mark to distinguish it from others on the stick. Use your stick to measure subsequent pots, so that you can make adjustments if necessary. Record the diameter of pot rims on your stick by using calipers to transfer the measurement.

Throwing guide

You can use one or more guides as you throw, which point to sections of the pot, such as the rim, a decorative line, or where a change in shape occurs. You can buy guides or make your own. Throw your first mug and set a stick in clay so that the tip is almost touching the rim. Carefully remove the mug from the wheel and throw the next ball of clay. Use the stick to show you the height and width of the rim required in the new mug.

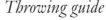

I find it difficult to pull handles from clay attached to the mug. What can I do?

Full-length handles

Fit full-length handles to your pots. Any mistakes you make in pulling the handles can then be easily discarded without ruining your pots.

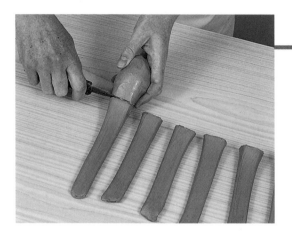

I. Pull handles that are long enough to fit your pots and set them aside until the clay firms up. Make a few more than is necessary, and lay them out next to each other so that you can choose the best.

2. When the handles are no longer sticky, but still have some spring, attach them to your mugs. You can butt the cut edge of the handle directly onto the wall, or smooth it into the pot as shown above. Score and slip the mug in both cases. Bend the handle into a flowing curve and join the other end to the pot, as shown on the right.

I do not like pulling handles. Can I make them in any other way?

You can make handles by rolling out a coil of clay. Most potters shape this kind of handle more by rolling it on a textured or patterned slab, or giving the coil a flatter shape. You can also form handles by pulling a coiling tool or shaped piece of wire through a lump of clay. Make molds of handles that you have taken from manufactured items, or that you have modeled yourself. Create a range of sizes and styles to suit your work.

Many of my handles split across during drying. How do I stop this happening?

Use less water when pulling your handles. If the clay becomes very wet, the handles shrink much more than the pots they are on, and so pull away and crack. If coiled or slabbed handles split during drying, use softer clay to form them. Clay that is too hard cracks under the pressure of bending into shape. Handles and pots need time to settle together before they start to dry to any extent. Cracking can occur when the handles dry too quickly. Wrap your pots in plastic sheeting or keep them in a cold, damp area for a day to slow their drying at this important initial stage.

Should I turn all of the pots I throw to make them lighter or even out the walls?

Use turning to create distinctive forms

When learning to throw, it is easier to reshape unsatisfactory pots by turning. It is better, however, to work at improving your throwing skills. Turning can be appropriate for forms that are impossible to make through throwing alone: wide-rimmed bowls that need extra support while the clay is wet, pots that require footrings, and forms that have sharply defined angles, for example. The danger in turning all of your pots is that you may remove the vigorous, thrown aspects and create clinical, lifeless forms. Try to finish shaping the inside of bowls while you are throwing rather than always rescuing a bad shape by turning. Using ribs when throwing helps to give shapes more definition while preserving a lively feeling in your work. Make use of turning when you want a pure, crisp shape – for example, when making translucent porcelain forms. In this case, the aim is to remove all traces of throwing rings and to give a perfectly smooth finish.

Above right: Elsa Rady, Lily – heavily turned to create a refined shape
Above left: Sandy Lockwood, Wood-fired, salt-glazed teapot – thrown and altered without turning

What tools do I need for turning?

Turning tool selection

There are several categories of turning tools, including stem tools, loop tools, and ribs. Stem tools have a shaped metal head, which allows you to pare the clay from the pot at different angles. They are particularly useful for sharpening the shape of footrings, galleries, and lids. Loop tools cut the clay away very effectively, and are helpful for removing large amounts of clay. They are less likely to cause chattering. Sharp metal ribs are good for final shaping and for smoothing the surface of the clay. They can give a precise finish to straight edges and curves. Ribs can also cut decorative features as you are turning. All of these tools can be bought from clay suppliers, but you can also make a wide selection yourself. Fashion loop tools from banding saw, hacksaw, or jigsaw blades, bent and strapped to a handle. Cut kitchen and decorating knives and scrapers to useful shapes, and use a surform blade as an effective turning tool.

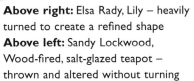

How do I know when my pots are dry enough to turn?

Pots are ready for turning when they are firm enough to hold their shape, and do not distort too readily when picked up. Some potters turn their pots when they are still on the wet side of leather-hard. This produces vigorous turning marks, which almost become part of the throwing. Others turn drier pots, to create clean, precise forms. Turn your pots at different stages to find your personal preference.

How do I make sure my pot is in the middle of the wheel for turning?

Tap the pot

Tapping the pot onto the center of the wheelhead in a few quick moves is the most efficient way of positioning the pot for turning. Although it may take some time to learn, it is worth persevering with this method. Once you have the knack, you will be able to replace pots easily whenever you need to examine their shape.

1. Wet the wheelhead and place your pot as centrally as you can by eye. Start the wheel moving, and if you see a side of the pot bulging out as it turns, tap this area sharply with your hand. The bowl should move a little nearer to the center. Keep your other hand poised ready in case the pot flies from the wheel.

Drawn circles

Use the circles etched into the wheelhead, or draw your own circles as a guide when positioning your pot. Move the pot until it is an even distance from the circles around it. It should then be in the middle of the wheelhead.

When I try to turn my bottles, they fall over. Is there a way to hold them onto the wheel more securely?

2. If you are successful at hitting the bulge, several times and with just the right amount of force, your pot will move onto the center of the wheelhead. Give the base of the pot several taps to make sure that the water creates a seal between the wheelhead and bowl, and it is stuck firmly enough to commence turning. Always keep one hand around the pot during turning in case the pot is suddenly released.

Make a chuck

You can support your awkward pots inside leather-hard, dry, or bisque-clay chucks. These should be thrown in the shape of squat, solid vases with flaring necks. A chuck with no base allows you to make use of both ends, which can be shaped to accommodate different-sized pots.

Bisque chucks may need to be soaked in water before use. Center the chuck on the wheelhead first, then lower your bottles into it for turning. You may find it necessary to hold your pot in place with soft clay.

How can I attach my pots to the wheel for turning without pushing the rim out of shape?

Use lumps of clay

This is the first method of attaching clay to the wheelhead that most potters learn. Place your pot upside-down on the wheelhead and press lumps of clay around the rim, so that the pot is held tightly. Be careful not to push the rim out of shape.

Tap on-center

With this method of holding your pot, a thin layer of water bonds the rim to the wheelhead. Very little damage is done to the pot; the rim may need a quick wipe with a sponge after turning.

Throw a clay ring

You can attach your pot to the wheelhead by making a clay ring, which will hold the pot in place and protect its rim. Throw a flat layer of clay across the wheelhead. Center your pot on top of this and mark around the rim. Remove your pot and either cut away the ring of clay outside the line, so that you are left with a circular pad of clay for your bowl to sit on, or cut away the central area to leave a ring of clay that will enclose the rim of your pot.

Throw a clay hump

Thrown humps of clay make useful supports for pots that are being turned. This is a way of holding bowls which are too big to rest on the wheelhead. Center a solid lump of clay, making its diameter fit the inside of your bowl. Place a piece of thin cotton or strips of newspaper over the hump, avoiding any large folds or creases. This stops your bowl sticking to the wet clay. Place your bowl on the hump and adjust its position until it is central. You can now turn the excess clay from the base of your bowl. The hump of clay can be reworked for turning different-sized bowls.

When I try to turn my pots, the walls push in. What am I doing wrong?

Blunt tools push into the clay and make turning difficult. Keep your tools sharp so that they cut through the clay cleanly. X-acto knives, or scalpels, that have changeable blades, and loop tools that are self-sharpening make efficient turning tools. Sharpen your stem tools on a wetstone, a grinding wheel, or a garden scythe sharpener.

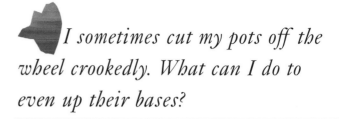

It is difficult to start turning a pot that was cut off the wheel with a jagged edge. How can I smooth it?

Remove unwanted clay

You must remove the ragged clay so that it does not have a detrimental effect on your turning.

USE A NEEDLE

Cut away the unwanted clay with a needle or sharp-pointed tool. Start a little way down the wall of the pot and cut up at an angle through to the base. This removes the corner section between wall and base, taking the jagged edge with it.

GRATE THE CLAY

Surform blades are good at removing irregularities in the clay. Hold a surform blade against your pot, and you will see the rough edges grate down to a smoother shape.

I sometimes cut my pots off the wheel crookedly. What can I do to even up their bases?

Make a level base

You need to work on removing the highest points of clay to level out the base of your pot.

1. As the wheel is turning, hold a sharp-pointed tool over the base of your pot so that it cuts ridges into the highest areas of clay.

2. With a flat-stemmed tool or loop tool, turn away a layer of clay. Start in the middle and work outward toward the edge, only cutting clay from the ridged areas as you progress. Repeat these actions several times until the base of your pot is flat.

3. Alternatively, you can use a serrated kidney to help you smooth the base. Create ridges in the clay by holding the kidney against the base, then even these out by rubbing a smooth-edged kidney over the area.

When I am turning my pots, little ridges appear. Why does it happen, and how do I get rid of them?

Smooth them out

The ridges that sometimes appear on pots being turned are referred to as chattering. They usually indicate that the pots are too dry to turn, that tools are blunt, or that you are not holding your tools firmly enough. Stem-turning tools that have a long, flat side most often produce chattering, especially if they are heavy and cumbersome in your hand. Loop tools are far less likely to cause this problem.

1. To clean up chattering on your pots, cut ridges across the affected area with a pointed tool. A loop tool with a serrated edge can also be used successfully.

2. With your tool resting on a smooth area, gradually cut away the ridges of clay. As you move across your pot, your tool has a level support and therefore is not drawn into the up-and-down course of the chattering.

I want to make footrings on my pots, but I always turn through the bottom. How can I tell when I have turned enough clay away?

Bowl shape

You must have a picture of the inside shape of your bowl impressed on your mind, so that you can echo this, and not make a more extreme shape, on the outside. Keep taking the pot off the wheel to examine the inside shape. You can feel areas of thickness by holding the wall of the pot between a finger of each hand and running the two fingers down the pot in unison. Look directly down onto the wall and you will see where your fingers are pushed wider apart by a thick area of wall and come closer together on a thinner section. The distribution of weight in the bowl also usually tells you where more clay must be removed.

Use a thumbtack

Push a thumbtack, or drawing pin, into the center of your pot on the inside. Any hole left by the thumbtack easily heals over. Turn the center of your bowl until you feel the very tip of the thumbtack. You must be very attentive when turning to detect the tip as soon as it appears, so that the thumbtack is not pushed out or dragged through the clay. Remove the thumbtack, and use the depth you have reached as the lowest point of your turning.

The footrings on my bowls are always too wide. How can I gain more control of the shaping?

Turn from the outside

Turn the outside of the footring first, so that you can determine its width. You will have greater control if you always work from the outside to the middle.

1. Look at the profile of your bowl and take away clay from the edge of the base. You are aiming to create a flowing line down the wall and through the footring.

2. When the outside of the foot is the right size, remove clay from the base. Leave a good thickness for the footring, and again work toward the middle to remove the remaining clay.

Turn upright

Alternatively, place your bowl on the wheel the right way up. Turn clay away from the base until you achieve the desired profile. Then place your bowl upside-down on the wheel and remove clay from inside of the footring.

My large plates sink in the middle during firing. What can I do to prevent this?

Support the center

Large plates need to be a little drier than other pots when you turn them, so that you do not push the middle area down as you work. Leave a button of clay in the center of the plate. This will act as a support to stop the plate sinking during firing. Make sure this button is the same height or slightly lower than the footring.

A second footring

Alternatively, give additional support to your plate by using a second footring on the base. Position it near the middle of the plate, and make sure it is no higher than the outer footring.

I like to make a deep footring on my bowls, but the thick clay sometimes cracks before I turn them. What can I do?

Throw a clay coil
You can make a footring for your bowl by attaching a coil of clay and throwing this to the right shape.

1. Throw and turn a bowl with a rounded base. Score and slip the bowl and attach a thick coil of clay. Take care to smooth the new clay into the bowl without trapping any air.

2. You can now throw a footring from the coil of clay, shaping it to complement the bowl. Turn the footring if you wish, when it is leather-hard.

Throw separate parts
You can throw a large footring or pedestal as a separate piece and join it to the bowl when the two are leather-hard. This allows you to throw the bowl with a normal thickness of clay at the base.

1. Throw a bowl and footring separately. You must learn to judge what size and shape of footring suits different kinds of bowl. Leave both until leather-hard.

2. Turn the base of the bowl and cut away any excess clay on the footring. Score and slip where both will meet.

3. Smooth the footring onto the bowl, using a slow wheel to help you adjust its position. Turn the footring if the shape needs tightening up.

THE DECORATION OF pottery can take many forms, from

enhancing the textural qualities of the clay to creating a

complete covering of brightly colored patterns. It is possible

to decorate pottery at every stage, from soft clay to fully

glazed ware, depending on the materials and techniques

used. It is in this area, perhaps more than any other, that you

can stamp your own style and character onto your work.

Decorating

*I would like to decorate my pots
without adding any color or glaze. What do
you suggest?*

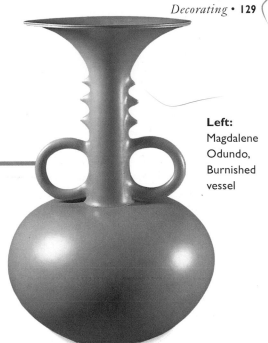

Left:
Magdalene
Odundo,
Burnished
vessel

Develop texture and form

There are countless ways to add interest to your pots by texturing the surface,
cutting away shapes and patterns, or incorporating modeled clay.

SURFACE TEXTURE

Create an overall effect or highlight
focal points with contrasting rough
and smooth areas. Introduce regular
or intermittent marks by scoring,
scratching, and scraping with a variety
of tools. Make repeat motifs by
pushing objects such as Lego bricks,
bottle tops, and plaster stamps into
the clay. Carve a pattern into a
cylinder or wheel of plaster, clay,
rubber, or plastic to create a tool for
rolling a band of decoration onto
your pots. Materials such as lace,
leaves, tree bark, and twisted cord
leave attractive textures when
pressed into damp clay. Experiment
with some of the endless possibilities
to develop your own style.

BURNISHING THE CLAY

The natural qualities of the clay can be brought out
by burnishing, which compacts the surface and
deepens the color. Work with clay which is free
from coarse particles. When the pot is leather-hard
to dry, polish the clay with a smooth pebble or
metal spoon to produce a soft sheen.

FILIGREE WORK

Cutting shapes out of a formed pot is known as
filigree work, and this can produce a strong
character that has no need of additional color or
glaze. Cut shapes to create a decorative pattern, or
a scene such as a landscape. The rims of bowls can
be shaped to add to the effect.

ADDED CLAY

Modeled decoration is a
good way to create highly
individual pots. Incorporate
molded sprigs or modeled
forms made from the same
clay as the body of the pot.
Sprigs are generally applied
to create repeat designs on
one or several pots.

Right: Kenneth Bright,
Sprigged bread crock

How do I make sprigged designs that are easy to replicate again and again?

Molding the sprigs

Sprigged designs are usually repeated around a pot or on many pots, so it is necessary to use a method that will yield the same design many times.

A SIMPLE PRESS MOLD

A press mold of decorative features can give highly detailed sprigs. First select the design for your sprig. You can model this in clay or use one face of a found object. There are two ways of making a simple mold: push the design into plastic clay and bisque fire the slab, as shown here; or make a one-piece plaster mold. Use designs with a low relief, so that the clay sprigs release from their mold easily.

CARVING A SPRIG

Scrape a sprig design into a block of plaster, using a knife, small chisel, or sharp metal tool. Plaster that is newly set and still fairly soft is easy to carve. Begin with simple shapes, but with practice you will be able to make intricate designs with this method. Remember that the clay sprigs will be a reverse image of the design in the plaster.

My sprigs are ruined when I pull them out of the mold. How do I stop them sticking?

Check that there are no undercuts or jagged lumps in your mold that the clay may be catching on, and carve or sand away any obstructions. Dust the mold lightly with talc between each sprig, checking that you do not leave a buildup of powder anywhere. This will help to lessen the effects of moisture deposited by the clay. When the clay is in the mold and you have removed any excess, push a lump of wet clay, a wet spoon, or a curved piece of plastic onto the back of the sprig. Pulling on this attachment should release the sprig cleanly from the mold.

My sprigs often crack away from my pots in the firing. How can I join them more successfully?

Create a seal between pot and sprig

Your sprigs should have a slightly convex shape to reduce the chance of trapping air as you position them on your pot. The pot should be no drier than leather-hard, and the sprigs must be as wet as possible, so that they can take on the shape of the pot wall without cracking.

I. Scratch and slip the back of the sprig and the area of pot where it will fit. Attach the sprig with a rolling action, starting at one edge and pushing the sprig firmly as you proceed. This will expel all of the air between the pot and the sprig.

2. Run a wooden tool around the join. There is less likelihood of cracking if you leave a clean-cut edge to the sprig and do not try to smooth the extra clay gradually into the pot. Drying your sprigged pots slowly also helps to prevent cracking.

How can I neaten areas where I have drawn incised patterns or cut shapes?

Use cellophane
To prevent the clay forming into little burs as you incise it, draw through a piece of cellophane or tissue. The design will be softer in appearance, but you will not be bothered by unwanted fragments of clay.

Brush burs away
To solve the problem once it has happened, do not attempt to clean up the decoration while the pot is wet. Once the pot is drier than leather-hard, brush the burs away with a soft brush. A small vacuum cleaner will do the same job by sucking up the fragments. Neaten cut areas further with a wet brush.

When I wipe my work with a sponge, my decoration is destroyed. What should I do?

Leave your work until it is dry. Then you can smooth it without obliterating the detail. Work with the finest sponge you can find — not those used for wiping down benches, which are generally coarse and holey, and leave marks in the clay. Soft, wetted brushes are a better choice for cleaning up intricate areas.

How can I break fewer pots when doing filigree work?

Cut at the right stage
Pots for filigree work should be truly leather-hard; the clay gives the smoothest cut, and the pots are stronger at this stage than when dry. Keep spraying the clay with water to keep it in the right condition to work on. A sharp X-acto knife (scalpel) is the best tool to use. Dip the blade in cooking oil to help it slip through the clay smoothly.

How can I enhance the modeling on my pots?

Above: Nicolette Savage, Tulip urn

Plan a contrast
Create a contrast with an oxide, a colored stain, or a shiny glaze. Brush a wash of color onto the modeling, then wipe with a wet sponge. The color will remain in the indentations and highlight the modeling.

I would like to decorate tiles with a raised texture as well as color. What techniques can I use?

Using waxes

There are several different ways in which you can use the resist properties of wax to produce decorative tile designs. Different techniques are used for unfired clay and bisque tiles.

DRY, UNFIRED TILES

Draw a design onto a dry clay tile, using a strong, melted wax or shellac – water-based waxes or latex will not work. Once the wax has set, keep washing over the surface of the tile with a wet sponge. The clay of the tile gradually washes away, but the wax remains, and the design will stand out from the surrounding area.

BISQUE TILES

On bisque tiles, use wax to draw outlines, so that you can paint on colored glazes in separate sections. Add a dark oxide or stain to the wax to give your tiles the effect of stained glass windows.

Decorate with slip

Slip will go on your tiles as a slightly raised design. You can draw outlines, or produce entire patterns by drawing, sponging, and stenciling with colored slips. Here is one exciting way of creating individual tile designs.

1. Throw a clay disk on the wheel. Try to make the clay flat, so that the tile will not have a concave or convex shape. You can make ring or spiral indentations in the disk.

2. Fill several slip trailers with differently colored slips. Turn the wheel at a fast speed, and squirt slip onto the clay. The slip will immediately spread out to the edges of the disk as it is affected by centrifugal force. Keep changing from one slip color to another, so that an intricate pattern is created. You can control the flow of slip to some extent, by altering the speed of the wheel and the consistency of the slip, but each design will be unique.

3. When you are happy with your design, cut the disk off the wheel and set it to dry. You can leave the decorated disks as circular tiles, or cut them into squares when leather-hard.

I like using red earthenware clay, but the color dominates any decoration that I add. What techniques work well with this clay?

Textured effects

Work with the color of the clay by using texture to decorate it. Create interesting surface contrasts with incised, impressed, and burnished areas to show the color of the clay at its best.

Above: Morgen Hall, Ice-cream dishes – the red clay body is covered in blue slip, which bleeds through the white tin glaze to create a mottled effect. Further motifs were applied using colored stains

Below: Daphne Carnegy, Majolica tableware

Opaque coatings

Use red clay for its good throwing and handbuilding properties, but disguise the color with an opaque coating. A slip can be used when the clay is leather-hard and an opaque glaze on bisque pots.

SLIP DECORATION

Opaque slips that have a light color stand out on red clay. Simple areas of slip that contrast with the body color can be effective, and sgraffito and slip trailed decoration work well.

MAJOLICA WARE

You can cover the body color of your clay completely with a coating of slip or opaque glaze. This gives you a ground on which to paint decoration in brightly colored stains. Earthenware pots that have highly colored brushwork on an opaque white tin glaze are known as majolica ware.

I am nervous of drawing on my pot with a brush. Which brushes are best for decoration and what is the best way to start?

Brushes for interesting marks

The best brushes hold a good amount of color, so that the marks you make flow freely. They include Chinese and Japanese brushes, special lining brushes, and square-cut and round shaders. Many of the brushes designed for watercolor painting are also suitable. Ceramic material will wear the brushes more quickly than paint or ink, however, so it is worth trying nylon, squirrel, and hog bristles as well as the more expensive sable brushes. Look for brushes that make unusual and interesting patterns: shaving brushes, pastry brushes, and toothbrushes are some examples.

Practice on paper first

Practice on paper, using watercolor paint or ink. Experiment to discover the sort of marks you can make with each brush. When you start to gain a rhythm in your painting, it is time to move on to a pot. Continue to work with watercolor, exploring the curves made by the walls of your pot, and the different way that the paint performs on the clay surface. Change to ceramic materials to give the pots their permanent decoration when you feel confident.

I want to decorate my pot by brushing colored shapes onto it. Do I have to do this at any particular stage?

Color can be brushed onto pots at every stage, depending on the materials you use. All of the coloring materials are made from oxides, but different additives dictate their application. Oxides mixed in water can be used on unfired greenware, bare bisqueware, and bisque that has a coating of unfired glaze. Some stains are formulated for use on greenware and under a glaze on bisqueware, while other stains can be brushed on top of the unfired glaze. You can mix these stains with a medium, with transparent glaze, or with water alone to create a range of effects. Both oxides and stains can also be utilized in the form of colored slips. Color can be painted onto fully fired glaze or vitreous clay, in the form of enamels or lusters.

Choose the methods that suit your style of decoration and your budget. Look for work that inspires you in books, magazines, stores, museums, and exhibitions, and try to find out the decorating techniques employed. This will give you a starting point from which to develop your own methods.

I want to make a more detailed drawing than a brush will allow. What can I use?

Underglaze pens

You can buy refillable decorating pens in a range of nib sizes and colors. They can be used on greenware and bisqueware.

Crayons and chalks

On bisque-fired work, use crayons and chalks, which are made from ceramic materials. Sharpen the crayons to give a fine outline, and smudge and blend the chalks to fill larger areas.

The brushwork on my bisque pots gets smudged when dipped into glaze. How can I stop this from happening?

Extra protection

Many potters give their decorated bisque pots an extra firing to about 1290°F (700°C). This is a high enough temperature to "harden" the oxides and stains, so that the brushwork will stay in place when the pots are glazed.

Alternatively, spray a thin layer of glaze over the decoration, using a diffuser or plant spray. This seals the colors, allowing you to handle the pots and dip them into glaze without smearing.

When I pack a glaze firing, I often smudge the decoration painted on top of the glaze. Can I prevent this?

Safeguard the color

Colors that are mixed with water alone smudge readily when painted on top of glaze, because the water quickly soaks into the bisque pot, leaving only a powder behind. Spraying a decorated pot with artist's fixative or hairspray helps to hold the powder in place. Adding some acrylic medium or gum arabic to the color helps the decoration to set onto the glaze, but color mixed in this way must be used up in one painting session. Design your decoration to allow blank areas where the pot can be handled. Decorate the inside of a bowl first, and you can hold the outside in your hands to reach all areas. Then complete the decoration by standing the pot on a banding wheel or whirler to paint the outside.

The glaze becomes powdery as it dries. Can I still paint on decoration?

Damp down a powdery glaze

Some glazes dry to a powder very quickly, while others remain smooth for a long period. A powdery surface tends to make brushstrokes drag and to suck up color from your brush before you can complete a stroke. Dampen the surface of dry glazes by spraying the pot lightly with water. Do not soak the glaze, or it will bubble away from the pot. Spray the pot at intervals during your work, if necessary. If you only want to paint a small area, wet that part of the glaze with a brush. A banded line around the top of a bowl, for example, may be more successful if you draw the line with a brush full of water first. This will soften the glaze enough to allow the color to flow smoothly.

Colors mixed with water sink into the glaze surface immediately. Combine the stain or oxide with a painting medium that allows the brush to move more easily. Glycerin also serves as a good lubricant.

When I paint on top of the glaze, it flakes away from the pot. Can I add anything to strengthen the glaze?

Use an additive

Adding gum arabic gives the glaze a harder surface. Use about 0.5 percent of the dry weight of material in your glaze, and make it into a solution with warm water before adding to the liquid glaze. A small amount of wallpaper paste or acrylic medium added to your glaze can also help it to stick to the pot more efficiently. Use your glaze within a few weeks of making these additions, or it will become moldy. Check that your kiln has adequate ventilation, since the new material will burn away, producing fumes.

Below: Jenny Clarke, Boxes – blue and green slips applied under a white glaze

My brushwork lines bleed into the glaze during firing. How can I stop this?

Stabilize the color

Oxides, particularly cobalt and copper, merge into the glaze, giving any lines a smudged appearance. Add china clay to make them more stable, using about half as much weight of china clay as stain. By adding clay to the coloring solution, you are actually making a slip, and your colors may become more muted. Colored stains are much more stable than oxides, and you may prefer to use these instead.

Choose the right glaze

How much a glaze moves varies according to the type of glaze and the firing temperature. Shiny glazes that are taken to the top end of their firing range can be very fluid, and any decoration on these glazes will run, so choose your glaze carefully to give your decoration a suitable surface. You may be able to improve existing glazes that are too fluid by lowering the firing temperature slightly.

If I put an opaque white glaze on top of underglaze decoration, will the colors come through?

Choose suitable colors

Most oxides will burn through an opaque glaze, giving an interesting mottled effect. However, only very dark stains, such as black and blue, can be used in this way. The resulting color will be a paler version of the stain or oxide, since the opacifier in the glaze affects the color. Black, for example, becomes a muted blue. You will need a thick application of color to produce a strong definition in the glaze.

Some of my oxides fire to an unpleasant, metallic black. How do I prevent this?

Oxide and glaze
Many oxides need to combine with a glaze to develop their true color potential. Copper and cobalt, for example, remain a dull metallic black if no glaze is present. Check that your pots do not have any raw patches where the glaze is missing underneath the metallic patches.

Use less color
Dense, metallic color can form in a glaze where an overload of oxide causes a burning effect, as in the three tiles shown above. Reduce the amount of oxide to produce a normal color response. It can be difficult to estimate how thickly a solution of oxide is lying in brushwork decoration, but assessment becomes easier with experience of working with these materials.

Make use of this effect
Glazes that have an overload of coloring oxide can be used to good effect on decorative and sculptural pieces. One such glaze, firing between 2190 and 2300°F (1200–1260°C), has a bronzed appearance, and is made from 12 parts red clay, 75 parts manganese dioxide, and 13 parts copper, mixed with gum arabic to help it adhere to the pot. Such glazes are very fluid, and you must protect your shelves from runs. Do not apply them to domestic ware, because the extreme quantity of oxides can seep into food during use.

Below: Steve Ogden, Caskets – the bronze glaze is created from an overload of oxides

Can I rewet stains and oxides that were mixed with water but have now dried?

Making use of dried colors
You can wet stains and oxides over and over again, since they return to their powder form when dry. Even when some glaze was used as part of the solution, you need only add water to make them serviceable colors again. Keep colors wet in small screwtop jars, but use Chinese inkstones and small bowls if you do not mind the color drying between painting sessions.

I only have a few colored stains. Can I mix them to get more shades?

You can mix glaze stains, body stains, and underglaze colors to make a range of subtle shades. Work with colors that fire to the same temperature for maximum success. Some of the colors are more dominant than others, and combinations will sometimes produce unexpected results, because of the oxides used in the manufacture of the stains. Test your mixes, therefore, before using them to decorate more important pieces of work.

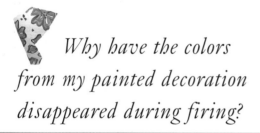 *What can I use to decorate my stoneware pots with bright red?*

Enamels and low-temperature glazes

You can use enamels (far right) and earthenware glazes (center) on stoneware pots to create a vivid red. To apply an earthenware glaze, fire your pot to your usual stoneware temperature, but leave the area that is to be red unglazed. Now paint this bare area with a red earthenware glaze and refire the pot to a low temperature appropriate for the glaze. You can add gum arabic to the glaze, or heat the pot to help it adhere. When using an enamel, leave the area unglazed at stoneware temperature if you want a matte red color. Glaze all of the pot in your stoneware glaze, and apply the enamel on top of the fired glaze for a shiny red. Fire the pot to 1380°F (750°C) to harden the enamel.

Glaze and body stains

In the last ten years, manufacturers have spent a lot of time formulating bright red colors to fire at stoneware temperatures, which is a traditionally difficult area. These are continually improving and it is now possible to buy glaze and body stains that produce a good range of reds (above left).

Why have the colors from my painted decoration disappeared during firing?

Some stains and underglaze colors are formulated for use at earthenware temperatures, and burn out during a higher firing. There is now a good selection of colors that will fire to stoneware temperatures, and you need to make an appropriate choice for your working methods. Certain glaze materials have a detrimental effect on particular coloring oxides. For example, any colors that contain chrome, especially pink stains made from a mixture of tin and chrome, turn a muddy brown, or burn out completely, when zinc is present in the glaze. Greens and blacks made from chrome become pink with the addition of tin. Become familiar with the ingredients of your glaze and colored stains, and work with those that give you a satisfactory response.

I decorate press-molded dishes with colored slip. How do I stop the dishes from collapsing as they take up water from the slip?

Use the mold for support

When your dish is leather-hard, neaten and finish the edges and base to your satisfaction. Return it to its mold to decorate the inside, as shown here. This will give it the necessary support to prevent it from collapsing or warping out of shape. After you have worked on the inside let the dish dry until the clay is firm before decorating the outside.

How do I make the tree-like patterns I have seen on slipware pots?

Mochaware decoration

Pots which have dark, tree-like patterns bleeding into a light-colored slip are called mochaware. The medium for creating this decoration is traditionally made by boiling tobacco in water and sieving the mixture to extract the juice. It is possible, however, to substitute another medium which has a degree of acidity, such as cider vinegar. Add a colorant of manganese dioxide, iron oxide, or black stain to your chosen medium. Pots decorated in this way should be fired at earthenware temperatures, so that the patterns have a strong definition.

1. When your pots are leather-hard, dip them into slip, leaving an area of uncoated clay at the bottom. The slip needs to stay damp as you create the pattern, so you may wish to finish decorating each pot completely before moving onto the next. White or cream slip is generally used, but you can experiment with other colors.

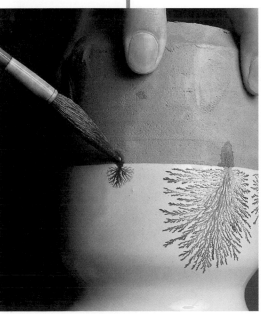

2. Holding your pot upside-down, apply your mocha solution to the uncoated clay with a brush. You can paint a band that touches the slip, or dot individual areas around the pot, as shown here. The color will fan out and spread into the slip. Apply more solution if you wish the pattern to travel farther. Wait until the liquid is set before turning the pot the right way up.

I use a slip trailer, but the lines of slip just run. What is wrong?

Check that your pots are not too wet to work on. Slip used on wet clay tends to sink in and merge with the background. If the clay is at the leather-hard stage, the slip lines take less time to dry and retain the raised effect associated with this type of decoration. Slip used for slip-trailed lines must be thicker than that for a flat coating. Thicken a slip that is too watery by adding CMC (carboxy methyl cellulose) until you achieve the desired consistency.

How can I make my lines of slip flow smoothly?

Slip trailers

Brushes are not the most suitable decorating tool to use with slip, because they cannot hold enough of the material. You can buy slip trailers from suppliers, which will greatly improve the quality of your decorative work. They are made in various sizes to give a range of line thicknesses, and they hold a reservoir of slip, so that you can produce a continuous line. Practice will enable you to create controlled patterns of vigorous designs, once you have mastered the pressure necessary to keep the slip flowing. Slip trailers can also be used for decorating with colored glazes. You can make your own slip trailers from throwaway plastic bottles.

What tools do I use for sgraffito work?

Bought and found tools

You can buy tools from clay suppliers that are specifically designed for sgraffito decorating. They include knives with shaped ends, and needles of different thicknesses, which produce a variety of lines and flat shading. You can also use items found about the home and studio to give unusual character to your designs. Knitting needles, forks, paint and plaster scrapers, serrated knives, lino-cutting tools, and small chisels are some examples to try.

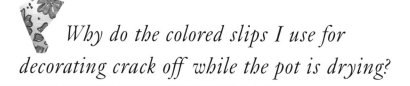

Why do the colored slips I use for decorating crack off while the pot is drying?

The consistency and shrinkage rate of the slip must be appropriate for decorating your pots. Add a little water to your slip if it is very thick, and try decorating your pots at an earlier stage, before they become too dry. When uneven shrinkage rates between the slip and the pot cause the decoration to crack, changing the clay, or the ratio of different clays, in your slip may be the only way to solve the problem. Experiment with ratios of ball clay and china clay until you find a mixture that works on your pot, or use the same clay for pot and slip, so that they are compatible.

What are vitreous slips?

Impervious decoration

Vitreous slips are slips fired to a temperature that bonds the materials into a very hard, impervious layer. Unlike ordinary slip, which allows water to soak into the pot, slips that are vitrified are usually the final decoration of a pot, with no covering glaze applied. Here are two simple recipes for vitreous slip.

Earthenware slip	
1830–2040°F (1000–1150°C)	
Dry porcelain	100 parts
Borax E. Frit.	35 parts

Stoneware slip	
2040–2300°F (1150–1260°C)	
Dry porcelain	100 parts
Feldspar	35 parts

When is the slip at the best stage to produce sgraffito decoration?

Clean-cut lines

The clay should come away smoothly and cleanly as you incise your sgraffito designs. Work on clay and slip that is leather-hard to create the best effects. If the slip flakes away in small chips, the clay is too dry. Use tools that are sharp and give a precise edge to your lines. If your tools move the slip, so that a ridge develops along the line you are scratching, the clay is too wet.

Below: Loretta Braganza, Textural slipware

I would like to decorate my slab pots with colored clay or slip in a lively way that contrasts with the very controlled slabs. What can you suggest?

Make slabs from colored slip

Incorporate freely formed designs of colored slip into your clay slabs. Energetic designs are more suitable for this technique than intricate details. Use slip trailers for linear patterns, or pour the slip for solid areas of color.

1. Build a wall of clay around a plaster bat. Make the wall a little higher than the thickness you intend your slabs to be. Create a pattern on the bat with different colored slips. The pattern will set on the plaster bat.

2. Pour prepared slip over the design, until it fills the entire bat and forms a flat layer. The clay walls will hold the slip in place.

3. Let the slip dry until you can remove it from the bat as a slab. The colored design will be intact on the underside. You can now use this decorated clay to build your slab pot.

Roll a slip design

Rolling out a slab of clay that you have decorated in slip can give exciting results. Apply the decoration to one side of the slab, then turn it over onto a plaster bat. Roll the back of the slab so that the clay is stretched. Your initial design will be manipulated, adding extra interest to the flat color.

Colored clay

You can make a pattern from pieces of colored clay and combine this into your slab to make pots with bold designs.

1. Apply a design of colored clay to a plaster bat, and roll a layer of your regular clay body on top.

2. This gives you a clay slab with a colored pattern on one side, which you can use to make slab pots, setting the colors on the inside or outside.

I would like to use colored slips to decorate my pots, but the coating I get from dipping or brushing is very dull. How can I make a more interesting surface with slips?

Textured slip

Coat a small section of a leather-hard pot with a thick slip – either colored or the same as the clay of the pot. While the slip is still wet, push a stiff brush, a broken brick, or crumpled foil all over the area to create a random texture. It is important to work on small sections, so that the slip does not become too dry to manipulate. When this coating of slip is dry, cover it with another layer of slip in a different color or with a wash of oxide or body stain. Let the pot dry completely, and sand or scrape the surface layer away to discover a pattern that resembles reptile skin.

Painterly effects

Apply the slip in innovative ways to create interesting results. Use different shaped and textured sponges to apply a variety of colored slips, or roll the slip on the pot with rags in a similar way to home-decorating techniques. These methods produce a surface with greater depth, as the different colors intermix and show through each other. You can also manipulate wet slip, with fingers or tools, so that the underlying body color shows through. Use this technique in a vigorous way to create an overall pattern, or designs that highlight particular areas of a pot.

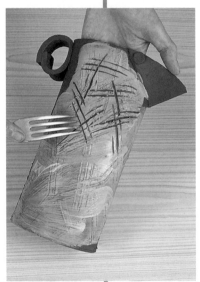

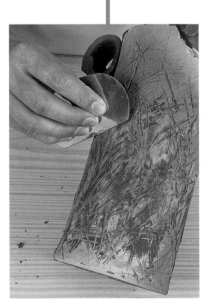

Scratch patterns

Texture the surface of the clay, so that colored slip settles in the indentations.

1. Take a leather-hard pot, and scratch or comb random marks over the area you want to decorate. Experiment with different tools to give you an array of interesting marks.

2. Paint a layer of colored slip over the indentations. When this is dry, scratch a pattern into the clay and cover with a differently colored slip. Build up several layers of slip in this way, scratching through each layer when it is leather-hard. Try to make your marks run in a different direction each time, so that previous layers are not obliterated.

3. Dry the pot until all of the layers of slip are completely firm. Scrape at the surface with a metal kidney and you will reveal an arbitrary pattern of intersecting colored lines.

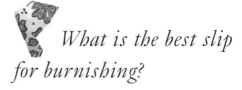

The lines of my incised decoration are not sharp enough. How can I improve them?

Work on firm clay

Clay that is too soft will not retain the sharp detail of incised lines when slip is worked on top. Choose a pot that is leather-hard to dry, and apply the slip to incised lines with a soft brush. Wait until the coating of slip and the pot have dried to a firm consistency before removing the unwanted material, so that you do not merge the colored lines into the background clay.

The right tools for the job

When incising designs, use a tool that cuts at 90°. Lines made from a V-shaped indentation thin out, and sometimes disappear, as you scrape the slip away. Use a scraper with a sharp edge to remove the excess slip cleanly and reveal the design. A metal kidney is ideal.

What is the best slip for burnishing?

Terra sigillata

Slip that gives the finest surface for burnishing is known as *terra sigillata*, and consists of only the finest clay particles. To make this slip, you must separate out different materials that make up the clay. Make a slip from a few drops of soda ash, powdered clay, and distilled water. Pour the mixture into a bowl or jar, and let it stand for 48 hours until the particles settle in layers, the heaviest at the bottom and the finest at the top. Pour off the water and use the top third of clay, which is an exceptionally smooth slip.

I have made some agate pots using mixes of colored clay, but the pattern is smudged. Can I do anything to make the colors clearer?

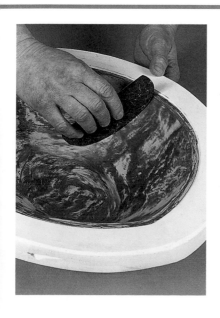

Uncover the pattern's potential

No matter what technique you use to make your agate pot, the surface is likely to show a very thin layer of body clay, or a surface whose colors have lost their definition because of sponging and smoothing of the clay. Take away the surface layer of clay and you will reveal the true potential of the pattern. Pots that are thrown can be refined as part of the turning process; and pinched or molded pots are easily scraped with a metal kidney.

Cutting across the pattern

You can make agate pots by slicing into the clay. Build a pot with very thick walls, and when it is leather-hard, reshape it, using a sharp knife or wire. Cutting across the lines of color in this way creates an agate pattern of very different character.

What techniques can I use to decorate my pot with a repeat motif?

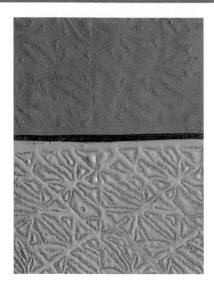

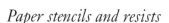

Sponge work

Use a shaped sponge to decorate with colored slips on greenware; with stains and colored glazes on bare bisque, or unfired glaze; and with enamels and lusters on fired glaze and vitrified clay. When using slip, you can apply a positive pattern by dabbing slip onto your pot (above left), or you can make reverse patterns by dabbing a dry sponge onto a layer of wet slip (below left). Experiment with sponges that have large and small holes, and with varying densities of foam.

Paper stencils and resists

Cut a simple shape in paper to use as a mask when you apply the color. There are also many paper shapes such as stars, dots, and rings, available in stationery stores. Using this method, your repeat motifs are blank areas, left untouched by color, giving a negative, clay-colored shape. To make your motif a positive shape, cut your design in paper, but use the outside area as a stencil. The stencils found in craft and interior decorating stores are suitable.

Ceramic paper shapes

Buy sheets of brightly colored transfer paper that has a surface coating of enamel from your clay supplier. The transfers must be used on glazed clay, and a smooth, shiny glaze gives the best results. Cut the enamel transfer papers into geometric shapes to make repeat motifs. Soak each in water until the backing paper slides off easily, and apply the shape straight onto the pot, making sure that the side that was affixed to the paper is now joined to the pot. Smooth the shape over to completely eliminate any trapped air or water.

I find it difficult to cut detailed designs in sponge. Are there any useful techniques?

Either freeze and cut, or burn out your design

The difficulty with cutting into foam is that it pushes away from you with each stroke of the knife. Draw your design on the surface of a sponge with waterproof ink. Wet the sponge and freeze it to give yourself a firmer ground to work on. Cut out the design with a sharp X-acto blade (scalpel). Glue your finished designs to a backing of cork, linoleum, or wood, so that they keep their shape. Alternatively, you can burn a design into your foam block using a hot wire or soldering iron. Remnants of upholstery foam serve well. Draw the outlines on the dry foam first to guide you as you work. BEWARE! Fumes from burning foam are extremely toxic and potentially fatal. Only attempt this technique if you are wearing an efficient respirator and the room has plenty of ventilation.

How can I achieve a crisp edge to sponged areas of decoration?

Block out areas of your pot that are to remain uncolored by brushing on a thick layer of latex. Let this dry, and apply a sponged layer of color. Peel off the latex to reveal blank shapes showing the color of the body clay. Brush latex onto the pot again, making new shapes, and sponge with a different color. Build several layers of color in this way to yield a pattern of overlapping colored shapes.

How can I stick my paper resist shapes down so they don't come away at the edges?

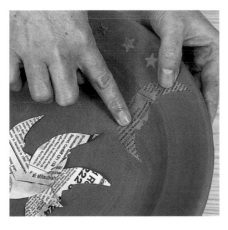

Working with resist shapes
On unfired clay, water is sufficient to keep thin, absorbent paper shapes in place. Work on a pot that is leather-hard; if it is drier, the clay will soak up the water too quickly. Place the paper shape on the pot and smooth it over to release any trapped air. Pay particular attention to the edges of your shapes. Sponge or brush a layer of colored slip onto the pot, taking care not to disturb the shapes. You can also dip, pour, or spray the color, so long as the clay or the shapes do not become oversaturated. On bisque or glazed pots, stick your shapes to the pot with a glue stick.

How long should I leave the paper resist shapes on my pot?

Take the paper shapes off when the slip, glaze, or colored wash loses its wet sheen. If you remove them too soon, the design will smudge. Leave them too long, and the dry layer of color may crack and peel away with the paper. Check that all color is firmly set before applying any new paper resist designs.

What is the best paper to use for resist work?

For greenware, you need a paper that is thin and absorbent; newspaper, florist's paper, or butcher's paper are suitable examples. You can use a variety of tapes and sticky papers on bisque and glazed surfaces, including masking tape, graphic design papers, carpet tapes, book-covering plastic, and bicycle tapes. These are easily cut to shape with a sharp blade. Preformed shapes, such as those made for children, and sticky labels are also suitable.

Is there anything I can use as a resist on my heavily textured pots?

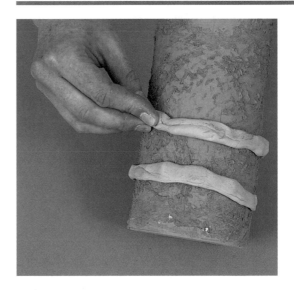

A modeling clay resist
Waxes, papers, and tapes do not work on such a disruptive surface. Modeling clay or Blue Tack makes a good resist on surfaces that are heavily indented. These products do not become sloppy when wet as regular clay would do, so you can remove them easily after decorating. Both sometimes leave a slight oily residue, which may resist patches of glaze or color wash.

How do I decide which type of wax is best to use on my pottery?

Choose a wax to suit your methods

Melted wax is the traditional resist used in pottery, but because of difficulties associated with preparing and applying this type of wax, many potters have turned to modern materials.

MELTED WAX

Melted wax is especially good on greenware, because it is unaffected by the moisture in the clay. It flows readily on bisqueware and unfired glaze, so it is excellent for brushwork decoration. This wax is unforgiving of mistakes on bisque, however, and any dribbles are hard to eradicate.

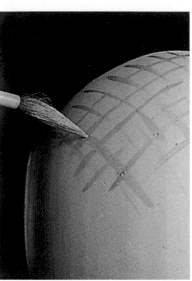

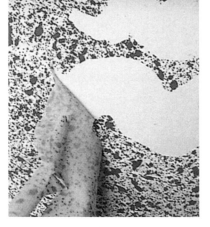

LIQUID WAX

Waxes based on acrylic materials are easy to paint on, and especially suitable for detailed work. These liquid waxes can be used for a variety of decorative techniques, such as sponging and spraying. They are not as strong as melted wax, and glaze or color usually remains on the surface of the wax, needing to be sponged away to complete the resist process. Liquid wax can be unreliable on greenware, because the moisture of the clay combines with the wax.

LATEX

Latex can be used on greenware, bisque, and unfired glaze. Its outstanding feature is that you can peel dry latex from a pot and apply more elsewhere. This allows you to build up and overlap color or glaze. The latex sold as an artist's material and latex in glue form are suitable for resist work, in addition to the brands made for ceramics. The brush clogs very easily with latex, and you must work quickly to avoid pulling off dry material as you apply the resist.

I would like to use a melted wax for brushwork. Which wax should I choose?

You need a wax which is not too brittle when cold and which flows smoothly without running off the pot. This usually means mixing waxes, and you can experiment with proportions until you find the qualities you prefer. A mixture of two wax candles with a half-teaspoon of paraffin, or equal amounts of candle wax and beeswax are two useful recipes.

How can I keep melted wax warm while I am working?

Maintain your melted wax at a good working consistency by placing it in the top container of a double saucepan. Pour some hot water into the bottom container, and keep it warm on a small gas stove or electric food heater. In this way, the wax is not directly over the heat, and should not become too hot. If the wax begins to smoke, however, it is overheating and could ignite, so remove it immediately. You can adapt many other heaters for use with melted wax, including electric frying pans and baby bottle warmers, and essential oil burners.

How can I protect and clean my brushes when using wax?

Brushes used with melted wax cannot be protected. Do not try to clean them, but take them out of the wax at the end of a decorating session, smooth the bristles to a point, and leave the brushes hanging bristles downward to keep a compact shape. Dip liquid wax brushes into dishwashing liquid or soft soap before each use to give them a protective coating. Clean them in hot water and more soap after use. Brushes used for latex can also be protected with soap. Remove the buildup of dry material frequently, and clean the brushes more thoroughly with turpentine.

My brushes are too clogged for drawing fine wax outlines that resist colored glazes. What should I use?

Special resists
Various glues that are released by squeezing the container can be used as tube liners to draw fine outlines. To make a drawing nozzle, cut a small aperture in the sealed top, or attach a piece of electric wire, with the metal core removed. You can also buy special resist pens from clay suppliers.

Ceramic wax application
Use a tjansing (batik waxing tool) or slip trailer for drawing fine lines. Mix a dark stain or oxide into the wax to give a black outline for decorative work that resembles stained glass designs. This is known as *cuerda seca*, and is a traditional method of embellishing tiles.

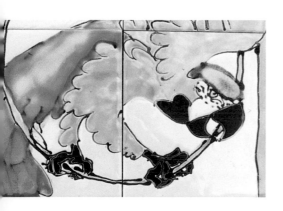

Left:
Bronwyn Williams-Ellis, *Cuerda seca* parrot tile

Can I use regular wax crayons as a resist, even on fired work?

Interesting results
You can use wax crayons as a resist, and by coloring instead of painting the wax, you will create a grainy texture. The color of some crayons leaves a mark on fired clay — notably high-quality artist's pastels, which

have a high percentage of pigment. The raw material that colors artist's products is often the same as that used in ceramic stains; it is the methods of manufacture and the additional binding substance that differ. Even some strong watercolor paints leave a residue of faint color on fired clay.

Is it possible to get rid of a run made in melted wax, or have I spoiled my pot for good?

Remove or refire
Melted wax can easily be scraped from unfired clay, and from unfired glaze with a little care. It is on bisque that removal of mistakes is difficult, because the wax soaks into the clay. First, scrape away all the wax you can with a sharp knife. Then rub the area with a cotton

pad dipped in paraffin, or burn the wax away with a blow torch. Often the only sure way of removing all traces is to refire the pot in the next bisque firing.

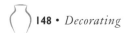
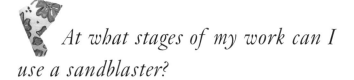

Can I add more decoration to a pot after a glaze firing?

Remove the glaze

Sandblast your pot to alter the surface of the glaze, and take away areas of glaze completely if you wish. With this technique, sand is blown against the pot with such force that it eats away at the glaze. Special equipment is needed to spray the sand and keep it enclosed as you blast. The effect on your glaze depends on the size of the sand particles, the softness of the glaze, and the duration of blasting. Using resists, such as masking tape or latex, you can create designs which show as a different texture from the unmarked glazed areas, or you can eradicate areas of glaze that were not successful.

Left: Russell Coates, Blue enameled dish

Add to the glaze

Some materials are specifically designed to go on top of a fired glaze. These include enamels, china paints, and lusters. You can also add a second glaze to introduce another color or a reactive texture as the different glazes melt together. Add gum arabic or acrylic medium to your second glaze to help it stick to the pot.

At what stages of my work can I use a sandblaster?

Experiment on work at all stages, from raw clay to fully fired ceramic. You need to change the size of the sand grains and the pressure of blasting when working on materials of differing strength. Softer clay is the most readily affected by the sand. Dry and bisque clay come away in larger fragments than those of glazed ware, so you must check and sieve the sand regularly.

I only want to sandblast specific areas. What can I use to mask the rest?

Masking tape, drawing or writing paper attached with tape, and adhesive-backed films are all adequate. The edges of papers and tapes wear quickly, so that the sandblasted area takes on a soft outline. Latex is another useful resist for sandblasting. The sand bounces off it with little wear to the blocked-out shape, so it gives a sharper definition than hard-edged resists, such as tape.

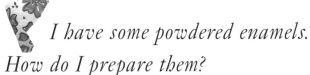

I have some powdered enamels. How do I prepare them?

Mix with a medium

Combine powdered enamel with a dedicated medium bought from your clay supplier. Put a little of the powder onto a flat sheet of glass, and add a few drops of medium. Blend with a palette knife, lapping and turning the material until it is thoroughly mixed. Start with a small amount of medium and add more if necessary to achieve a smooth consistency; your enamel must be thick enough to stay on the glazed surface, but thin enough to flow easily when applied. Add a little turpentine if thinning is necessary.

How do I apply enamels?

Using decorative techniques

Most decorative techniques can be used with enamels. The only additional problem is that you are usually working on a shiny surface, which can make applying color difficult. You can paint detailed designs and flowing lines with a brush or pen. Although a brush is suitable for larger areas, you may prefer to remove brushmarks by dabbing the area with a sponge until the color is more even. Spray the enamels with a small spray gun or airbrush to obtain a smooth application of color, or shaded effects.

Is it possible to make enamels and china paints less glossy?

Mix your enamel with a matching shade of underglaze color to create a more matte finish. Experiment with the amount of color you add to reach the surface quality you desire. Work the enamel and underglaze color together, using a palette knife on glass. Enamels and china paints that are painted onto a matte glaze or unglazed clay have a silky or matte texture. Paint particular areas of your pots with a matte glaze, or leave them unglazed, so that enamel decoration added at a later stage does not take on a full gloss appearance.

Why have my enamels gone black during firing?

Enamels that have gone black are overfired. Firing temperatures vary for different colors of enamel. Reds and golds, for example, usually fire lower than other colors. Check with your supplier the optimum temperature for your enamels. Add your decoration using several firings, if necessary, starting with the highest temperature and progressing to the lowest.

When my enamels and china paints are fired, there are small holes in the color. How do I prevent these?

A clean working surface

To prevent imperfections, you must keep your pots scrupulously clean. Cover the work with polythene while it is waiting to be decorated so that dust does not form on the glazed surface. Wear thin cotton or surgical gloves to prevent the transfer of even the slightest amount of grease from your fingers to the work. You can wipe pots over with turpentine or mineral spirits (white spirit) before you begin work to make sure that they are absolutely clean, but dry them thoroughly before you start your design.

I would like to liven up some plain glazed pots with luster. What techniques can I use?

Adding interest with lusters

Paint bands of metallic luster onto your pot, at the rim and neck for example, or coat areas with a pearlized luster to give more depth to the color. Use lusters to create intricate patterns on top of the glaze. Experiment with pale lusters on dark glazes for subtle effects, and strong pinks, blues, and metallic lusters on a white background for more dynamic designs.

Working with resists

Lusters shrink away from areas that have been coated with dishwashing liquid or turpentine. Use this reaction to create unusual networks of color.

1. Paint bands of different colored lusters onto a glazed pot. Experiment with a variety of color combinations and band widths. Allow the luster to dry until it is slightly tacky to the touch.

2. Using a paintbrush, dot small spots of dishwashing liquid or turpentine onto the luster. You will see holes and runs of color appear. Although this type of pattern can never be fully controlled, with practice you can learn to manipulate the materials to some extent and create more intricate or simpler networks of color as required.

Printed textures

Print lusters onto your pots using textured materials. You can choose to highlight a particular area or create an all-over pattern. Pour some luster into a flat dish and dip in some textured materials such as shaped sponges, leaves, or lace, or paint the luster onto the surface of the material. Press this against your pot to transfer the textured pattern.

Create marbling

Lusters float on water, just like the inks used for making marbled paper. An intricate pattern of colors created in a water bath can be transferred to the surface of a pot.

1. Fill a container with cold water, and add a little vinegar to help the colors break up. Drop different colored lusters onto the water, and swirl them about with a stick to create a marble pattern.

2. Dip a pot into the water bath, then pull it out smoothly through the surface film of luster. The marble pattern will cling to the pot as it emerges from the water.

Some of my lusters are very thick and sticky, while others just run off the pot. What should I do?

The thickness of liquid lusters, sold in bottles, varies according to how long they have been stored, the conditions of storage, and the quantity of medium that they contain. You will need lusters of differing consistencies depending on the techniques you adopt. Thin down very sticky lusters with a proprietary thinner to make it easier to work with. If the luster is too fluid, heat the pot before you start work. The luster will then dry quickly, before it can run too much.

My fired lusters rub off easily. Have I done something wrong?

First check that you are firing to the correct temperature. Underfired lusters do not melt fully, and can easily come off the surface of the pot. Alternatively, your glaze may be the problem. Not all glazes are suitable for luster work. The glaze must start to re-melt at just the right temperature. Too little melt and the lusters do not merge with the glaze properly; too much, and the glaze does not recover its normal texture after firing. If your glaze is not reacting properly, you must find a more suitable replacement.

When I fired lusters on my pot, they all came out a pinkish color. What happened to the other colors?

Pink is dominant
When working with lusters, keep the colors completely separate by using a different brush for each color. The pink/purple luster shades tend to dominate other colors, and all of your lusters can turn pink if contaminated with tainted brushes. It is also possible that you overfired your lusters. Most colors will become pink if the temperature is too high and they are beginning to burn out. Fire your lusters to about 1380°F (750°C) for a more satisfactory result.

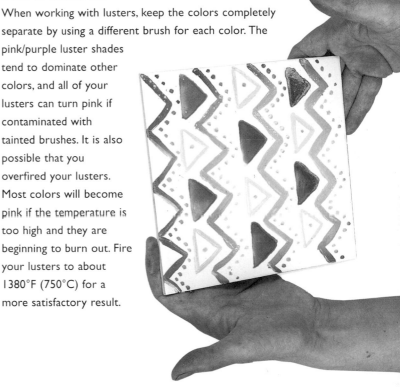

I find the lines of luster that I paint with a brush are too thick. How can I make very detailed designs?

Creating thin lines
Wet luster always spreads out on the glaze surface, so even a thin brushstroke can become unwieldy. Simple mapping pens, used for pen-and-ink work, give extremely precise lines and are easily dipped into the luster without clogging.

What happens if I put lusters on pots that do not have shiny glazes?

Creating colored sheens

On pots with a silky or matte surface rather than a shiny glaze, lusters produce a soft, pearly sheen instead of a bright metallic color. A thick luster can be especially drab under these conditions, but building up thin layers of color can create subtle results. Use underlying colors in the clay or as a slip to give depth to the decoration.

Right: Judy Trim, Mexican mauve lustered bowl

What are decals and how do I use them?

Printed designs

Decals are pictures or text printed onto a special transfer paper and coated in a gel called covercoat solution, which enables them to be used as transfers for decorating pottery. You can buy a wide range of ready-made decals, including flowers, animals, geometric patterns, children's subjects, and well-known phrases. You can also have your own designs printed as decals by a specialist company, or make them yourself using transfer paper and covercoat gel. In the teaset below, ready-made decals were used.

Below: Philomena Pretsell, Tartan pansy teaset

Working with decals

Most decals use enamels and are added on top of a fired glaze, but you can have artwork printed in underglaze colors for use on bisque and greenware pots. By using decals you can quickly create very detailed decoration, and use repeated motifs on a large numbers of pots.

1. To apply decals, cut up the sheets of printed paper, and soak the separate designs in water. The artwork, covered in a transparent coating, will fall off the backing paper. Place the decal onto a glazed tile or pot, making sure that the side which was sticking to the paper is now lying against the pot.

2. Smooth over with a finger or sponge to remove excess water and air bubbles. Allow to dry before firing to 1290–1470°F (700–800°C) to fix the design.

What printing methods can I use for transferring my designs to ceramic work?

Low-tech printing methods

There are several methods of printing traditionally associated with decorating pottery, such as sponging and using textured roulettes. The following two techniques use a minimum of extra equipment.

RUBBER STAMPING

Cut a design into a block of rubber or an eraser with a sharp craft knife. You can also buy ready-made rubber printing blocks from stationers, craft stores, and printers. Ink your rubber design using a sponge soaked in ceramic stain, or buy a special ink pad from your clay supplier. Press the rubber stamp onto bisque or dry clay to print the design.

LINO PRINTING

Draw your design onto a block of linoleum, and score the lines with a V-shaped cutting tool, chisel, or knife. If you have difficulty cutting, heat the linoleum to soften its surface. Take care to keep both hands behind the cutting tool, to avoid accidents. Roll a slab of clay over the lino block to transfer your design to the clay. You can also color the lino block with ceramic stains to add areas of textured color to the raised outlines.

Technical printing processes

Designs printed on ceramic tissue paper or decals are easily transferred to ceramic work. It is therefore possible to use all forms of printing techniques to create a design on paper first and then apply it to your pots, tiles, or sculptures. If you have the facilities to work with screen printing, including photographic transfer, lithography, and etching, very detailed representations and text are possible. Many ceramic manufacturers use these processes for decorating industrially produced items. When working with flat sheets of clay, such as for tiles or slabbing work, it is possible to print straight onto the clay, using silk screening, etching, and direct photo transfer.

I would like to use color in my clay sculptures. What methods can I use?

All-over color

When form is an important aspect of the work, any changes in color or added pattern can confuse the eye and detract from the overall shape. Many sculptors rely on a single color and texture to show a form at its best. You can use the color of the clay itself, and enhance this with burnishing and waxing, or coat your work in vitreous slip to change the color and texture. A complete coating of glaze, such as a celedon or metallic glaze, can often give the impression that a sculpture has been made from a material other than clay, such as jade or bronze. A more recent development are non-ceramic finishes, euphemistically known as room-temperature glazes, which are now being used and accepted more widely. These include acrylic paints, enamels, car paints, wood stains, and varnishes.

Highlighting details

Washing a dark oxide or stain into the cracks and crevices of a clay sculpture can highlight particular areas. In this way, colored details are unified by the dark lines, much like a pen and ink drawing or print, as shown here. Shading a color from light to dark can also help to give focal points more prominence.

Right: Wendy Kershaw, Ceramic clock

A GLAZE CAN transform a pot into a thing of beauty or ruin it irreparably, so it is essential to learn how to choose and apply such a finish appropriately. Ready-made glazes are widely available, but mixing your own gives greater scope for obtaining unusual surfaces. Combine well-chosen glazes with a knowledge of firing techniques, and you will have greater control over the final, vital stages of your clay work.

Glazing and Firing

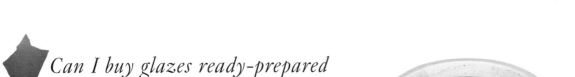

Can I buy glazes ready-prepared for use on my pots?

A full range of glazes

You can buy a wide variety of glazes from ceramic suppliers: glazes of different colors and textures, glazes for every temperature range, and glazes for particular kinds of firing. You can also choose how you wish to apply your glaze. Many are in powder form (far right), for you to mix with water; some are already mixed with water for spraying, dipping, or pouring (left); and others are blended to a thicker consistency for brushing onto pots (center).

How do I know what temperature of glaze to use on my pots?

Low bisque method

The usual method of firing studio pottery is to give the pots a first bisque firing at a lower temperature than the subsequent glaze firing. The pots remain porous after the bisque firing and you can apply the liquid glaze easily. Then you fire the pots to their highest temperature to mature the glaze and clay together. Before following this method, you must check with your supplier which clay you are using and the temperature range for firing it to optimum strength. You can then match your clay to a glaze of compatible temperature, choosing from: earthenware 1905–2100°F (1040–1150°C); mid-temperature 2100–2230°F (1150–1220°C); and stoneware 2230–2370°F (1220–1300°C).

Industrial method

It is possible to take your pots to their highest temperature in the first firing, and then fire the glazes to a lower temperature. In this way you can use earthenware glazes on clay that has been fired to stoneware temperatures, thereby combining the strength of the high-fired body with the clean, bright colors of low-fired glazes. The major problem of this method is the difficulty of applying glazes to clay that is no longer porous. Some potters overcome this by using spraying techniques and specially formulated glazes, and it is the glazing process that industry favors.

How can I tell which kind of glazes are the best to use? Which are the most useful?

Once you have decided on the temperature range of your glaze firings, there are a number of other factors to consider. Glazes can be transparent, translucent, or opaque. Transparent and translucent glazes allow the color of the clay and any slip, oxide, or colored stain decoration to show through. A clear glaze with no added color makes a versatile base, since you can add your own oxides, glaze stains, and opacifiers to produce a range of colored glazes. Opaque glazes cover the body color, and decoration is generally painted on top of the glaze. A white opaque glaze can provide a good base for oxide and glaze stain additions.

You can buy glazes that give different textures to your pots, from smooth and glossy, through satin and satin matte, to dry matte and heavily textured surfaces. Smooth, shiny glazes are ideal for domestic ware. Some of the satin finishes are also suitable, but you must take care to choose glazes that are not easily stained by food and marked by cutlery. Dry matte and heavily textured glazes create interesting surface qualities for decorative pots and sculptural work. Some glazes are formulated to work under particular conditions, such as oxidized, reduced, and raku firings, and this may be a factor in your choice.

What equipment do I need to mix my own glazes?

A basic selection

In order to mix glazes you will need some lightweight buckets or bowls that are easy to clean. If you plan to sieve your glaze, you need two containers. A lidded bucket, or a glass jar with top, is good for storing the prepared glaze. A sieve and stiff brush, or a mixer, is also necessary. Most potters sieve their glazes, so that the powdered ingredients are thoroughly incorporated into the water and no lumps remain. Some potters, however, prefer to use a glaze or paint mixer to amalgamate the wet and dry ingredients, because they believe that sieving takes the character out of glazes.

You need spoons, scoops, or cups to carry the dry materials, in a range of sizes that enable you to pick up large quantities of raw ingredients and small weights of oxides. Use accurate scales that can weigh tiny amounts correctly. Purchase a special beam scale or a balance with separate weights, as kitchen scales are not usually precise enough for weighing glaze materials.

How can I find out what materials I need to mix a glaze?

There are many glaze recipes in ceramics books and magazines, and also on the Internet. These list raw materials and the weights of each needed to make a particular sort of glaze. Many also describe the glaze qualities, and how additions will change the color or texture. These are a good starting point. Remember that you may not achieve identical results with a given recipe, because of differing clay body or firing conditions, so test small amounts before committing a large batch of material to a glaze.

Must I weigh the ingredients for glazes or can I use spoonfuls instead?

In a recipe for a ceramic glaze, the proportions of raw materials are calculated by weight. If you use spoonfuls of ingredients, you are working in volume. These are different methods of measurement, and you cannot interchange them. To see this for yourself, weigh out 2oz (50g) of whiting and 2oz (50g) of china clay. You will discover that there is much more china clay in volume – or spoonfuls – than whiting. If you are starting to formulate a glaze from scratch, and you are not following an already calculated recipe, you can use spoonfuls of materials if you prefer. However, this is a less accurate measure, and you may have difficulty keeping the glaze consistent.

How much water should I add to my powdered glaze?

Calculating the thickness

The clay you are using, the thickness and porosity of your pots, the kind of glaze, and the method of application all have a bearing on how thick your glaze should be. A starting point is to add between 1¾ and 2½ pts, or 4 to 6 cups (1–1.4 liters) of water for every 2lb 3oz (1kg) of dry material. Earthenware glazes are usually the consistency of thin milk, and stoneware glazes are thicker, like cream. Glazes for spraying (above left) will have more water than those for dipping and pouring. Brush-on glazes (below left) are thickest of all.

You can use thin glazes on very smooth clays, especially porcelain, but very sandy, textured clays need a much thicker coating. All these pointers will help you, but you must test glazes with your particular clay and firing conditions to achieve the best results.

My glazes never look the same as they did in the catalog. Why is this?

Conditions affect results

The pictures of fired glazes found in catalogs can only act as a guide to the color and texture of a particular glaze. They show how a glaze has reacted to one set of circumstances. The clay that you are using, your firing cycle, and the shape of your pots may all be different from those pictured, and will slightly alter your results. If you want to reproduce the glazes as they are shown in the catalog, find out as much as you can about their firing conditions, and make your own test pieces to discover the best way to achieve similar results.

How can I make sure that all my pots receive the same, even coating of glaze?

Keep stirring the glaze

Glaze material gradually settles to the bottom of the bucket. You must keep stirring your glaze to maintain a consistent thickness. The glaze used on the pitcher shown here was not stirred regularly, so it received a thinner coating than the bowl. Leave a stick in the bucket during a glazing session, so that you can stir the glaze regularly.

Examine your pots

Pots built from sandy clays often need a thicker glaze than those formed in a smoother clay. Arrange your order of working so that you use a thick glaze for pots in coarser clay, and dilute the glaze as you move on to smoother pots. The thickness of the walls can also affect the take-up of glaze. Thin areas are not as porous as thicker clay. Start by adding less water than usual to your glaze for coating pots with thin walls, and dilute the glaze for your thicker pots.

My glaze is never the same from one batch to another. How can I make it more consistent?

Measure the water content

Each time you mix a new batch of glaze, add the same amount of water for every 2lb 3oz (1kg) of dry material, so that the liquid becomes another measured ingredient in the recipe. You can then make each new mixture the same thickness. If you leave your glaze standing for weeks, some of the water will evaporate. You can use a hydrometer, which measures specific gravity, to keep the amount of water in the glaze consistent for reuse.

Bisque firings

Try to make sure that your bisque firings follow the same pattern each time, so that your pots have the same porosity. Pots that receive a higher or longer firing soak up less glaze, and this affects your finished results.

Raw materials

One factor that you cannot control is your supply of raw materials. As different areas, or different seams, are mined, the composition of materials can vary in subtle ways. Potters must learn to accommodate these slight inconsistencies when necessary – which is not very often.

How do I stop my glaze settling into a solid lump at the bottom of the bucket?

Add bentonite

Adding 1–2 percent of bentonite to your glaze helps to keep the particles suspended in the water without affecting the fired glaze quality. Do not attempt to mix the dry bentonite directly into your liquid glaze, because it will form unmanageable floating lumps, as shown here. Mix the bentonite thoroughly with the dry glaze ingredients before adding the water. Or, make the bentonite into a paste with some water. Gradually add glaze to the paste until it becomes a smooth liquid. Blend this into the bulk of the glaze.

Prevent settled glaze from hardening

Put a few drops of calcium chloride or magnesium sulfate into your glaze. This will stop any material that settles out of the water from forming a solid lump, so that you can stir the glaze back into suspension with ease.

My glaze has hardened at the bottom of the bucket. Can I reconstitute it?

Mix a little at a time

It is very hard work to mix a solid lump of glaze back into the water. Instead, drain off the liquid and break the cake of glaze into small pieces. Return the glaze to the water a little at a time, mixing each piece as you do so.

When sieving glazes, I find it difficult to hold the sieve firmly over the bucket. What can I use to help me?

Rest the sieve on supports

A sieve full of glaze can be heavy and unwieldy to hold in one hand while the other is working the brush. Place two sticks across the top of the bucket to support the sieve, and free your hand for pouring the glaze. You can refine this device by using two strips of strong wire. Bend the ends of the wire to clip over the rim of the bucket, and cross the wires over each other to form a seat for the sieve. Arrange the wires so that the sieve rests down inside the bucket, to prevent stray splashes of glaze from escaping.

I want to experiment with different kinds of glaze. What sort of test pieces should I make?

Throw test pieces

Thrown shapes are useful for testing, because they show how glazes perform on curved surfaces. Add indentations and grooves to the clay as you throw, to give you additional information.

MINIATURE POTS

You can make small bowls and vases quickly by throwing off a hump of clay. They let you see how your glazes flow on the inside and outside of a pot.

CUT A THROWN RING

Throw a large ring of clay. When it is leather-hard, cut it into small slabs to use as test pieces. Form a thick area at the base of the ring, so that each slab can stand up, allowing you to test your glazes on a vertical surface.

Rolled slabs

Small slabs of rolled-out clay are helpful for initial testing of glaze mixtures and for flat colors. They are limited, however, because they do not show how glazes move on a vertical or curved pot wall. Bend clay slabs to form shapes that are more useful for testing glaze reactions.

My glazes have not come out like my test pieces. How can I make the initial tests more reliable?

Precise measurements

When mixing test glazes, make your measurements as exact as possible. It is not easy to work with very small amounts, but the slightest alteration in proportions of the different raw materials can affect the color or texture of the glaze. You must use very accurate weighing scales to achieve successful results. Small cup sieves help when mixing the ingredients.

Informative pieces

Apply the glaze to your test pieces in the same way as your pots. Make test pieces whose shape and texture will give you plenty of information about your glaze, such as how it moves on a curved or vertical surface, how it pools in indentations, and how textured surfaces show through. Try out different thicknesses of glaze by double-dipping, brushing, or spraying. You can also test how colored slips, stains, or

oxides work with your glaze. Small test kilns can give you quick results, but they do not fire your glazes under normal conditions. Test pieces fired alongside your work give you a better indication of how new glazes perform in your usual firing cycle. This is an excellent way of filling the small spaces between pots when firing a full kiln load.

What is the most efficient way of using my glaze?

Brushing

Brushing is the most efficient way to apply a small quantity of glaze to a pot, because every last drop can be used. Glazes for brushing tend to be thicker than those for other methods. Add 2–3 percent CMC (carboxy methyl cellulose) to help the glaze flow smoothly.

Spraying

When spraying, you need less glaze to cover the pot than when dipping, but you lose a quantity of glaze that falls wide of the pot. Spraying the glaze gives a more even coating than brushing.

Pouring and dipping

To pour and dip, you need a generous amount of glaze. However, there are ways in which these methods can be made more efficient. Pour the inside of pots by filling them only halfway. As you pour the glaze, roll the pot around in your hands to give the inside a complete coating. To cover the outside of pots, place them on sticks over a bowl and pour the glaze around the top of the form. The glaze runs down and coats the surface of the pot. Dipping the outside of a pot gives a more even coating than pouring, but you need enough glaze to submerge the pot. Reduce the amount of glaze required by using suitably shaped containers. For example, a tall pot can be glazed in a thick pipe that has one end sealed off; and a flat plate can be rolled through glaze in a garbage-can lid.

How do I glaze the inside of vases, mugs, and pitchers?

Pour glaze in and out

The inside of cylindrical forms is usually glazed first. Pouring the glaze in and out in one smooth, rhythmic action leaves an even coating. You can then glaze the outside by dipping, pouring, brushing, or spraying. Never hold a pot by the handle for glazing, since this can cause cracks or breaks.

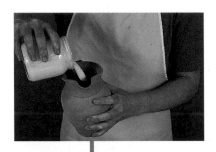

1. Pour glaze into the pot until it is about half full. Work quickly, so that the glaze does not soak into the base of the pot too much.

2. Take the pot in both hands and turn it in a smooth motion, letting glaze pour out as you do so. The glaze rolls around the inside of the pot to form an even coating. Aim to release all of the glaze just as you meet the starting point of your turn. No area should be left bare or given a second layer of glaze. Finish draining the pot with a flick of the wrist, to dislodge the last remaining drips.

The inside of my pot has a good covering of glaze, but the outside is thin. How can I improve this?

As you glaze the inside of your pots, the clay soaks up water. If you immediately try to glaze the outside, the clay is too saturated to hold enough liquid to give an adequate coating. After glazing the inside, leave your pot to dry overnight. The outside will then take up a good covering of glaze to give you better results.

My fingers get in the way when dipping the outside of pots. How do I correct this?

Cover bare marks

Your fingers will inevitably leave patches of unglazed clay when you hold a pot and dip it from the rim to the base in a single operation. Hold the pot as close to the base as you can and use the fewest fingers necessary for a good grip. Paint over bare fingermarks with a brush dipped in glaze, and scrape any lumpy areas when the glaze is dry and powdery.

Avoid fingermarks

Glaze your pots in a way that leaves no bare areas. As you pour glaze from the inside of your pot, dip the top section into the glaze. When this is dry, hold the pot by the glazed rim area, and dip the bottom into the glaze. Make sure that the glazed parts meet, so that the pot is entirely covered.

How can I cover up blemishes, such as fingermarks, in my glaze?

Cover thin or bare areas with dabs of glaze on a finger or brush when the glaze is still damp, but wait until it is dry before attempting to smooth thick areas. It is easier to scrape glaze away from fingermarks and dribbles when the glaze is powdery. Use a sharp X-acto blade (scalpel) or ridged fettling tool to remove excess glaze, and then smooth over with a finger. Some glazes heal blemishes more readily than others. Fluid glazes even themselves out as they move over the pot. If you cannot obtain satisfactory results with a viscous glaze, it may be worth trying an alternative.

The line where the glaze overlaps always spoils the look of my double-dipped pots. What can I do?

Fettle dry glaze

Leave the glaze until it is dry and powdery. Use a sharp, pointed blade, or a ridged fettling tool to scrape away the excess glaze. Dry glaze is easier to remove than glaze that is still damp. Be sure to wear a mask when fettling dry glaze.

Prevent an overlap

Use wax to prevent the glaze overlapping when your pot is dipped for the second time.

1. Paint a strip of latex or liquid wax on top of the glaze close to the edge of the first dip. Leave a tiny amount of glaze showing at the edge – about ½in (1mm) – to be sure that the second dip meets the first.

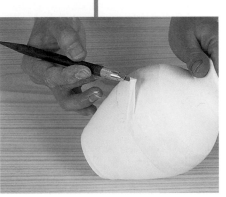

2. Dip your pot into the glaze a second time, to cover the lower section. Peel off the latex or sponge over the liquid wax to remove any excess glaze.

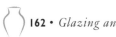

What is the best method of dipping bowls into a glaze?

Bowls with footrings

Bowls that have good footrings can be dipped in a single movement. Hold the footring in one hand and dip the bowl into the glaze and out again in a continuous rolling action. You need to twist your wrist around to its fullest extent in order to coat the bowl completely. Make sure the bowl points downward as you lift it from the glaze, and give it a firm shake to remove any drips left at the rim.

Large bowls and bowls with flat bases

Bowls that are too big to manipulate comfortably at the base, and those without a footring, can be held at the rim for glazing. If you do not want to disturb the glaze at the rim, dip your bowls in two halves and remove the central overlap of glaze to produce a smooth finish.

1. Holding the rim area with two fingers of each hand, roll the bowl through the glaze to coat the entire surface, as shown in the above sequence. Keep the bowl moving throughout, to create an even covering of glaze.

2. Dab glaze onto any bare patches left by your fingers. When the glaze is fully dry, fettle lumpy areas with a sharp X-acto knife (scalpel) or fettling tool until the surface is smooth.

How do I glaze difficult bottle shapes?

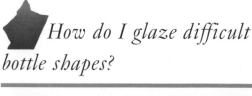

Use a funnel for support

Bottles that are too tall to dip into your bucket of glaze can be coated successfully by pouring. Glaze the inside first and let the pot dry. Insert a funnel into a small, narrow neck before turning the pot upside-down for glazing. This gives it more stability. Stand the pot and funnel on two sticks over a bowl to catch the excess glaze. Placing everything on a whirler, and turning the pot as you pour the glaze, gives a smoother coating.

I have made a complete mess of glazing my pot. What can I do to save it?

The best thing to do when the glaze has not coated a bisque pot successfully is to wash away all traces of glaze and make a fresh start. Make sure that you dry the pot thoroughly before attempting to reglaze it. Drying could take several days.

Are there any tools that can help me hold my pots for glazing?

Glaze tongs

Glaze tongs, available from clay suppliers, hold pots between two points, allowing you to dip without leaving fingermarks. Using the tongs to grasp the pots securely as you maneuver them through the glaze takes some practice. You can make similar tools from bent wire, or by attaching two nails to wooden tongs.

I try to brush on glazes, but they soak into the pot too quickly. What can I do?

Preparing the glaze

A glaze that is too thick will soak into the bisque clay too quickly. Try adding more water to the glaze, and brush it onto the pot in two or more coats to build up an adequate thickness, instead of applying a single layer. A few drops of CMC (carboxy methyl cellulose) also improve the consistency of the glaze. Dampen the bisque pot a little so that you can make a good sweep of the brush before the glaze soaks in.

Tools for the job

Apply the glaze with a wide, soft brush that carries a generous amount of liquid. Place your pot on a wheel or whirler so that you can move it as you brush and build up a working rhythm.

Can I use the same glaze for spraying as for dipping?

Glazes for spraying must have extremely fine particles, so that they do not clog the tips of spray guns and airbrushes. Pass your glazes through a very fine sieve, and grind any material that is left behind. Add some water to the glazes you use for dipping or pouring, as they need to be thinner in order to spray well.

The glazes that I spray onto my pots never seem thick enough when fired. How can I correct this?

Allow time for spraying

Glazes used for spraying contain a high proportion of water and can quickly saturate the clay. Spray in short bursts, so that the clay has time to soak up the glaze before more is added. If the clay is particularly thin or easily saturated, heat up the pot, so that it will take a thicker layer of glaze.

Testing the thickness

The appearance of a sprayed surface makes it difficult to judge how thick a layer of glaze has been applied. While you are gaining experience with this method of glazing, it is helpful to measure the thickness of the sprayed material with a pin. Test several areas to assess the evenness of the coating.

Is there any way I can spray glazes, without spending a lot of money on spray equipment?

Spray systems for all budgets
Systems that consist of a spray gun and compressor can be costly, but they produce an excellent surface. There are several bought and adapted alternatives that you can use, although these give a less perfect finish. Whatever equipment you choose, remember that spraying fills the surrounding air with glaze particles, so wear a mask, ventilate your work area, and extract contaminated air.

Small spray units
Small spray guns and airbrushes that run from cans of compressed air are particularly suitable for work containing fine detail. These are available from art and other specialist suppliers. Look out for canisters that do not contain CFCs.

Textured spraying
Spray or spatter glazes onto your pots with a toothbrush. Fill the brush by dipping it into the glaze. Hold it close to the pot and draw your thumb or a stick over the bristles to release a spray of glaze. To direct the glaze onto the pot and not over yourself, drag the bristles back toward you.

Adapted sprays
Handheld sprays designed for watering plants can be used to glaze your pots. The mouth-operated diffusers that artists use for spraying fixative or colors also work for spraying glazes and colors, but you must be especially alert to the risks involved when your mouth is part of the equipment.

What special effects can I get from spraying the glaze?

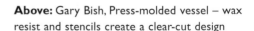

Left: Peter Lane, Mountain skies vessel

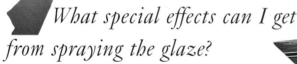

Quality of glaze
Spraying allows a more even coating of glaze than dipping, pouring, or brushing. This is especially important for intricate work, where too thick an application of glaze can obliterate detail. Spraying makes it possible to concentrate color in precise areas and to achieve smooth gradations of color, as in the example shown here. Areas of sprayed color can be soft and hazy, or glassy and flat.

Above: Gary Bish, Press-molded vessel – wax resist and stencils create a clear-cut design

Using resists
To create a sharp outline, you can use paper, tape, or wax resists. Waxes can also be sprayed on. Spray the wax onto a bare pot before adding the glaze, or between layers of glaze to create interesting surface textures.

Some of my pots stuck to the kiln shelf. How can I prevent this from happening in the next firing?

Remove glaze from pot bases

All areas that touch the kiln shelf must be free of glaze. If glaze melts between the shelf and the pot, the ware will stick to the shelf and removal can ruin both.

 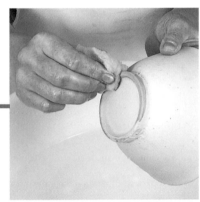

1. Wax the bottom of your pots before dipping them into the glaze, so that the coating does not cover this area. After glazing, give the area a quick wipe with a damp sponge to pick up any stray droplets of glaze.

2. Alternatively, after the pots have been dipped in glaze, wipe the footrings and bases with a sponge and water until they are free of glaze. Change the water frequently to make sure that you do not leave a weak coating of glaze behind.

Rest pots on supports

Stand earthenware items that are completely glazed on stilts and trivets. The sharp points stick into the melted glaze and break off when you separate pot and stilts, but resulting rough areas can be sanded smooth. This method of supporting ware is only suitable for low-temperature firings, since stoneware pots would slump around the stilts.

When you are using very fluid glazes, rest the pots on a slab of unglazed clay. These "sitters" protect your shelves from damage, but you may need to cut pots from their sitters if the glaze flows excessively. Help to catch oozing glaze by marking lines or indentations around the base of the pot. Wipe off excess glaze above these lines, and any flows will be slowed when they run into them.

My bisque firing went over temperature. How should I apply the glaze?

You may need to thicken your glaze with some additional material to help it stick to your pots. Mix a little gum arabic or CMC (carboxy methyl cellulose) with water until it forms a paste, and gradually add this to your glaze. Acrylic medium, used by painters, works equally well, and you can mix it directly into a bucket of glaze. Be prepared, however, for this to give off fumes during the initial stages of firing. Pots that have overfired are less porous than regular bisqueware. You can help to counteract this by heating the pots before glazing.

Some of my pots have raw patches of clay. How do I make sure this does not occur?

Take extra care

Once you have bisque fired your pots, you must take care that they do not become contaminated with dust or greasy fingermarks. Handle them as little as possible, and only with clean hands, and wash dusty pots before you glaze them.

Sometimes glazes that contain a high proportion of certain materials flake away from pots. Colemanite is particularly prone to this, and replacing some or all of it with a different flux, such as cornish stone or a frit, may solve your problem. Exchanging part or all of the ball clay for china clay, or calcining some of the clay material before mixing it into the glaze, can also help.

My glaze is too runny when fired. What can I do to correct this?

Replace some of the quartz or flint in your glaze with china clay and it will melt less readily. Also try firing your pots at a slightly lower temperature – say, 50–60°F (10–20°C), or one cone, below your present temperature.

My glaze is too viscous when fired. How do I improve the melt?

Replace some of the clay content of the glaze with quartz or flint to make your glaze more fluid. Also try adding a secondary flux, such as zinc oxide, or a frit. Firing the glaze 50–60°F (10–20°C), or a cone, higher will cause the glaze to melt more effectively.

My pots have little blisters in the glaze. How do I prevent them forming?

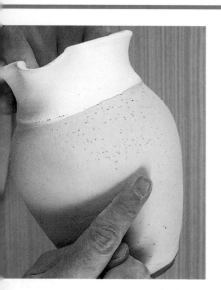

Preventing blisters
All glazes blister as the materials combine, but most have time to melt over as part of the firing cycle. Give your glaze a 30-minute soak at top temperature to allow the glaze to heal. If this aggravates the problem, the blisters may be caused by overfiring; turning the kiln off at a lower temperature may be the answer. Glazes mixed for dipping often contain tiny air bubbles. You can sometimes see these on your pots, where they appear as indentations in the unfired glaze. Footrings and appendages are areas particularly likely to catch these trapped air bubbles. Rub the dry, powdery glaze to fill in the holes, and your glaze will have a smoother surface when fired.

How can I make my transparent glaze opaque?

Opacifiers for your glaze
There are several brands of opacifiers that you can add. Mix them into your transparent glaze to obtain the degree of opacity you want. Use up to 8 percent tin oxide or 5 percent zirconium silicate to produce a white glaze. Tin is more expensive than zirconium but gives a softer, more subtle white. Additions of zinc oxide or titanium dioxide create a creamy, speckled opacity. All of these oxides are likely to change the nature of your glaze – making a more fluid melt, or changing the color response, for example – so test the effects before applying them to a kiln load of work. The test pieces above show the different effects that one glaze has on a variety of clays and with a green stain added. Transparent glaze was used on the pieces on the left, while 8 percent tin oxide was added to the glaze used on the right.

My transparent glaze goes cloudy in areas. How do I prevent this?

Transparent glazes look milky and sometimes take on a purple tinge where they are applied too thickly. This often happens in the bottom of bowls, where excess glaze has pooled. To prevent this, do not leave your pots in the glaze too long when dipping, and scrape away any excess glaze before firing. Underfiring can also cause clouding. You may be able to see tiny bubbles in the glaze which are causing the opacity. Fire the glaze a little higher, or soak it for a period at the end of the firing cycle.

Is it possible to lower the firing temperature of my glaze without spoiling it?

Changing the firing temperature may alter characteristics of the glaze that are important to you. Try adding a small amount of frit, lithium carbonate, petalite, or zinc oxide to your glaze ingredients. Replacing any feldspar or cornish stone content with nepheline syenite often reduces the firing temperature by one cone. The effect of any of these ingredients on your glaze depends on the other components, so you must test the results.

I had to turn off my kiln before it reached temperature. Can I now fire it to its normal temperature?

If the kiln was switched off well below the proper firing temperature of the glaze, the heat work from this first firing would have been negligible, and you can refire the work in a normal firing cycle. If the kiln was already close to the top temperature of the glaze, and had perhaps had a soak at this temperature, a great deal of heat work would have been done. Firing to your normal temperature would then overfire the glazes, and choosing a lower temperature to fire at can only be guesswork. In these circumstances, the best option is to try a temperature 70–105°F (20–40°C), or one cone, lower than usual.

Some glazes have a very narrow temperature range, and firing beyond or below this by only a few degrees ruins the surface completely. Other glazes have a wide firing range, and it is possible to fire across several cones without spoiling the surface. With these less temperamental glazes, you can refire work without problem.

I find my colored glazes very flat. How can I make them more interesting?

Color responses
Glazes that rely on the addition of stains for their color are consistent. Add a coloring oxide, such as copper or cobalt, to give speckles and flashes of color – or a texturing oxide, such as rutile, titanium dioxide, or zinc oxide. In an oxidized firing, combine ingredients, such as nepheline syenite, dolomite, or barium carbonate, to give interesting color responses. If you are able to fire with a reduced atmosphere, this will bring a whole new set of color responses and combinations to your work.

Above John Calver, Stoneware dishes

When I added coloring oxide to my transparent glaze, it ran down the pots. How do I color my glaze without this adverse effect?

Materials and temperature
The coloring oxides that you added to your glaze acted as a flux, and caused it to melt at a lower temperature. Glazes that have reacted in this way may also craze. To counteract this, add half the weight of coloring oxide in china clay to your glaze. Also try adjusting the firing temperature 70–105°F (20–40°C), or one cone, lower than usual, so that the glaze is not overfired.

Can I make a pink glaze without using colored stains?

Mix raw materials

Produce pink glaze by combining certain raw materials. For example, chrome turns pink when tin is present in the glaze; particular mixtures of dolomite and rutile give pastel pinks; and nickel and barium together produce vivid pinks. Using such reactions enables you to achieve pinks of a very different character from those due to colored stains.

The black glaze that I make using black stain is lifeless. How can I give it character?

Creating textured color

Replace some or all of the black stain with coloring oxides to create speckling and flashing in place of the even color. A mixture of any three of the following oxides produces a black: cobalt, copper, chrome, manganese, and iron. Use the qualities of particular oxides to add color highlights to the black: cobalt for blue, copper for green, and manganese for purple. Introduce textural characteristics by including raw materials in your glaze, such as barium carbonate, nepheline syenite, dolomite, rutile, and titanium dioxide.

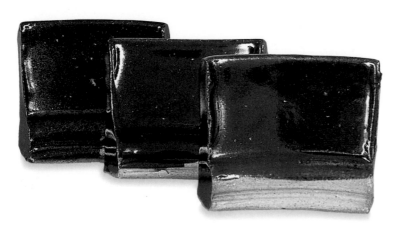

The glaze I am using has lots of specks and irregularities in it. How do I make a smoother color?

Coloring and texturing oxides are reacting in your glaze to produce irregular surface qualities. Work with glazes that produce a smooth surface, and use color stains rather than oxides to obtain a flat layer of color.

My glazes made with cobalt are a stark blue. How can I tone down the color?

Coloring oxides

Cobalt oxide used on its own is a powerful and vibrant colorant. Use the carbonate form to produce a softer gray-blue. Mix cobalt with iron, rutile, or manganese to create varying shades of gray-blue through purple-blue: 0.5 percent cobalt oxide plus 2 percent iron oxide – or 0.5 percent cobalt oxide plus 6 percent manganese or rutile – are typical additions.

Reactive glazes

There are raw materials that react with cobalt to break up the color and produce textural effects. Follow a recipe that contains nepheline syenite or barium carbonate – or add tin or titanium dioxide to your glaze – to create a more interesting and textured color response.

My white glazes are spoiled by specks of color. How can I stop this?

Check that all of the equipment you use for mixing white glazes is thoroughly clean. Any oxides remaining from previous mixes can show as specks in fresh glazes. Having two sets of equipment – one for colored, and one for white glazes – is a useful solution. White glazes can also take up specks of color when pots covered in colored stains are dipped into a bucket of glaze. Prevent this contamination by firing colored decoration onto pots before they are dipped, dipping glazes before painting on decoration, or applying the glaze by spraying. Some clays contain particles of iron that are large enough to bleed through the glaze on firing, causing brown flecks over the surface. Choose a lighter colored body, or coat pots in a white slip before firing, to eradicate this speckling.

Some of my white glazed pots come out of the kiln with green shadows on them. What causes this?

Copper contamination
Pots with copper in their glaze were placed too close to your white glazed pots. Copper volatizes during firing, particularly above 2190°F (1200°C), and transfers to surrounding glazes that are near enough to pick up the green color. It even moves through thin walls of pots to produce green areas on white or transparent glazes. To make sure that your pots do not become contaminated with copper, leave several inches between white and green glazed ware, or fire copper glazes on a separate shelf.

When I mixed some chrome into my glaze to make green, the color came out pink. What happened?

Reactive ingredients
Your glaze contains tin oxide. A combination of chrome and tin creates pink and not the usual green. Sometimes, although pots containing chrome remain green because there is no tin present in their glaze, pink areas appear on surrounding pots that are coated in a white tin glaze. You can use this color response to good effect in creating subtle decorative shadows. Even black stains that are created from a chrome base can turn pink under a tin glaze. If you want to eliminate the problem, use zirconium silicate instead of tin, or choose a different green colorant for your glaze.

Can I substitute one type of feldspar for another?

Potash feldspar, soda feldspar, cornish stone, and nepheline syenite are to a large extent interchangeable as the major flux in a glaze recipe. Each of these brings its own particular characteristics to a glaze, however. For example, nepheline syenite slightly lowers the melting temperature of the glaze, and results in a softer, more satin surface. The melting point of cornish stone is marginally higher than that of feldspar, but it has a greater resistance to crazing. Soda feldspar produces a markedly different color response with copper than potash feldspar does. Your choice of flux can therefore create subtle changes in the texture, firing temperature, and color response of your glaze.

Can I glaze unfired pots?

Glazing unfired clay is known as raw glazing, and produces once- or single-fired ware. Glazes used for raw glazing must have a high shrinkage rate, and many glazes that contain over 25 percent of clay are successful. Changing the china clay content to ball clay also helps the glaze fit. As you fire your pots, remember that you are combining the bisque and glaze stages, and begin by raising the kiln temperature slowly until all of the steam and impurities are driven out. You must expect a greater loss rate, but your firing costs will be reduced by this method.

 ## How should I apply raw glazes?

Clay dryness

Glaze your pots at different stages of dryness to discover the best time to apply the glaze. Some clays glaze perfectly when bone dry, and others need to be leather-hard to accept the moisture without bloating. After glazing the inside of pots, let the clay dry before coating the outside. The clay is then less likely to bloat from oversaturation. Check that all pots are thoroughly dry before you put them in the kiln.

Consistency of glaze

Most raw glazes are thicker than those for bisque use. Glazes that are thickened with CMC (carboxy methyl cellulose) work well when applied to dry pots. If your clay does not accept the take-up of water during dipping and pouring, apply the raw glaze by brushing, or by shaking a coating of powder glaze over the work.

 ## Can I make earthenware vases waterproof?

Earthenware-fired clay is not vitrified and is still porous. Give earthenware pots a full coating of glaze to make them waterproof. Do not use glazes that craze, because liquid will seep through the cracks.

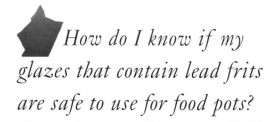 ## How do I know if my glazes that contain lead frits are safe to use for food pots?

Glazes formulated with lead frits are manufactured according to safety guidelines. If you are mixing your own recipes, make sure you do not overload this material and never add a colorant which is copper- or cadmium-based. These oxides cause lead to be released into food. A simple test for lead release is to half-fill a pot with vinegar. Leave for 24 hours, and examine the glaze surface under a magnifying glass. Safe glazes show no change, whereas those that release lead have matted surfaces. Potters selling domestic pots should have their lead glazes scientifically tested. Ask your supplier for information on laboratory testing.

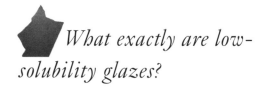 ## What exactly are low-solubility glazes?

There are two categories of earthenware glazes: leadless and low-solubility. Low-solubility glazes contain lead, in the form of a frit, which has been manufactured within safety guidelines. You can use these glazes on functional items, as long as additional colorants do not affect their safety.

How can I stop my glaze from crazing?

Crazing is caused by the glaze shrinking too much for the clay. The best solution is to find a different glaze recipe that is compatible with your clay. If you are determined to work with the glaze that you have, one or more of the following methods may help create a better fit.

Fire to a slightly different temperature. Both overfiring and underfiring a glaze can cause it to craze. Do not open the kiln too soon, because cold drafts on hot pots cause even well-fitting glazes to craze. Apply the glaze in a thinner coating – thick areas of glaze are more prone to crazing, especially on very smooth clays such as porcelain.

Another option is to adjust the recipe to include ingredients with a lower coefficient of expansion in the glaze. Add a little more flint and clay, or introduce some zinc, borax frit, talc, magnesium carbonate, or lithium carbonate. Replace potash feldspar with cornish stone. You can also use a clay with a higher silica content, or add flint, quartz, or prepared cristobalite to your usual body.

I have found a glaze that does not craze on my clay. How can I be sure it will not craze in the future?

Sometimes glazes that appear to fit well when removed from the kiln craze several months later. This can certainly be a problem on functional ware. Test your glazes for craze resistance by taking a pot from a hot kiln and plunging it into cold water. Use a range of temperatures from 250 to 320°F (120–160°C). Glazes that do not craze at 320°F (160°C) have good craze resistance, while those that craze at 250°F (120°C) are likely to do so within a few months of normal use.

Crazing and crawling are glaze faults, but can they be used as decorative effects?

Above: Gill Bliss, Female form

Lines of contrast

Make the lines of a crackle glaze stand out by using a strong, contrasting color. Apply ceramic materials, such as oxides, stains, and lusters, and set these into the glaze with a separate, lower firing. Permanent drawing inks, which do not need an additional firing, are suitable for decorative pieces. Cover the entire area of glaze in ink, and rub away the excess to leave a network of colored lines, as in the example shown here.

Crawling glazes

When a glaze separates into lumps and beads, instead of forming a smooth coating, it is called a crawling glaze. Dusty or greasy areas of a bisque pot can repel the glaze and some underglaze colors have the same effect. Some glaze ingredients, including zinc, colemanite, and opacifiers, are prone to crawling, especially when applied thickly. Crawling can be used to create startling lines of contrast between pot and glaze and a heavily textured surface.

Right: Gary Bish, Spheres '88

I want to make some interesting glazes for my decorative pieces. What ingredients should I use?

Glazing for textured effects

The glazes on decorative pieces need not meet the requirements imposed on functional ware, so you can experiment with a wide range of textures to enhance the mood or form of the work.

Dry and matte glazes

Glazes that have a high clay content fall between a slip and a glaze in texture, giving a dry surface. Red, brown, and buff clays produce colored glazes, which can be modified by adding coloring oxides and stains. White or cream clay lends lighter, pastel shades to added color. Large amounts of barium in a glaze give a matte and textured surface. Copper and cobalt are particularly useful colorants for barium matte glazes.

Right: Emanuel Cooper, Pitcher with barium matte glaze

Crater glazes

Some mixtures of ingredients create such a disturbance that the surface does not heal over during firing, and large craters, or eruptions, remain in the finished glaze. Add more than 0.5 percent of silicon carbon to produce a crater glaze. Layering glazes often results in unusual mixtures and intriguing surface qualities.

Left: Lucie Rie, Crater-glazed bowl

I have seen pots with crystals over the glaze surface. How are they produced?

Crystalline glazes

These are known as crystalline glazes, and the crystals grow from particular glaze ingredients, especially zinc oxide. A controlled firing cycle is needed to produce this effect. When the top temperature is reached, cool the kiln to 2020 or 1830°F (1100 or 1000°C). Hold this temperature to allow the crystals to form. With practice, it is possible to manipulate the firing cycle to create different sizes and patterns of crystal growth.

Above: Elsie Blumer, Crystal-glazed bottle

How do I stop my crystalline glazed pots sticking to the kiln shelf?

Use sitters

All crystalline glazes are fluid and likely to melt over the bases of pots.

1. Prepare for this eventuality by throwing a sitter for each pot to protect the kiln shelves from damage.

2. The fired glaze often sticks a pot to its sitter. Separate them by etching around the joint with a glass cutter and snapping them apart. Sand sharp edges of glaze with a carborundum stone to create a smooth finish.

Why are the tops of my pots bare of crystalline glaze after firing?

Crystalline glazes melt so readily that they flow down the pot during firing. To redress this, glaze the neck and rim areas with a thicker layer than the lower sections. The glaze will even out, giving a good overall coating to the finished pots.

I have started making pots in porcelain. Can I use stoneware glazes?

Glazes craze more readily on porcelain than on many stoneware clays. Test your stoneware glazes on your new pots to see if any fit well. Apply the glazes more thinly on porcelain than on stoneware. Celedons and glazes with a silky finish often make beautiful porcelain glazes, and you can find recipes specifically formulated for porcelain in magazines and books. Always experiment with test pieces first, because performance can vary in different porcelains.

Can I use the glazes I have oxidized in my electric kiln on pots to be reduced in a gas kiln?

Results will differ

You can use the glazes in an oxidized or reduced firing, but you will find several differences in your results. The heat work in a reduction firing tends to be greater than that in an electric kiln, and you may need to lower the firing temperature or accept altered qualities in the glazes. Many coloring oxides produce different colors in a reduced atmosphere. For example, copper turns red instead of green, as shown by the two tiles here.

I have heard of glazes that will give reduced effects in an electric kiln. What do I need to make these glazes?

Local reduction glazes

You can use ingredients that cause a reduced effect within the glaze, although the kiln itself has an oxidized atmosphere. These are known as local reduction glazes. Add 10 percent of carbonizing material, such as powdered charcoal, graphite, or ash, to glazes containing copper or iron to produce copper red and celedon colors in your electric kiln. You can also combine 0.3 percent silicon carbide with other glaze ingredients to make a local reduction glaze. In the examples shown above, 1.5 percent iron oxide and 2 percent bone ash were added to the green glaze, and 0.5 percent copper oxide and 1 percent tin oxide to the red glaze.

My reduced glazes have a gray cast in them. What caused this?

When the kiln is reducing, pots are surrounded with smoke. If the atmosphere starts reducing at a low temperature, some of the smoke can be trapped in the glaze, causing shadows on finished ware. This is called a "carbon trap," and some potters use it as a decorative effect. To prevent these gray casts, do not begin your reduction until the kiln temperature is above 1830°F (1000°C).

How can I achieve greater consistency in my copper red glazes?

Learn by experience

Copper is very volatile in a reduction firing, and it is more likely to float around the kiln atmosphere than to stay exactly in place. Sometimes areas of pots glazed with copper lose their color for no apparent reason, and at other times, marvelous rich reds emerge. Gaining an understanding of how your particular kiln performs, how your glazes develop in different parts of the kiln, how packing the kiln affects glaze qualities, and the advantages of different firing cycles are all part of learning to work with reduction glazes.

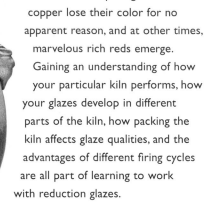

Left: Steven Hill, Reduction fired urn

How do I obtain color in my salt-glazed work?

Salt glazes are transparent. You can give your salt-glazed work color by adding oxides and stains to the clay body, covering the clay in a colored slip before firing, or adding color to the salt that you introduce into the kiln. Add oxides and stains to clay and slips in the usual way. The transparent salt-glaze deposits allow the various colors to show through. Slips that include 15–35 percent flint are excellent for this work, because the high silica content encourages a good layer of glaze to form. Use china clay, ball clay, nepheline syenite, and feldspar to make up the remaining ingredients. Porcelain slips also produce a good depth of color.

You can mix colorants with the salt that you introduce into the kiln for vapor glazing. Manganese dioxide and manganese chloride produce violet purples and red glazes. Copper sulfate gives turquoise; and copper carbonate creates a copper red glaze, provided a reducing atmosphere is maintained. The disadvantage of this method is that the colorants can leave deposits on kiln walls and around fire boxes that affect later firings.

After a salt firing, the insides of my pots were left bare. What happened?

The insides of cylindrical and lidded pots do not cover well in a salt firing. The vapor glaze produced cannot move around these areas easily. Glaze the insides of the pots separately with a compatible stoneware glaze before they go into the kiln.

How do I make raku glazes?

Low-temperature glazes

It is the nature of the firing process that creates the qualities associated with raku ware. The glazes used are simply earthenware glazes that melt at low temperatures of about 1650–1870°F (900–1020°C). Raku glazes usually contain very few ingredients: alkali, lead, or borax frit, combined with about 10 percent whiting and 10 percent ball clay, are typical examples. Additions of 5–10 percent tin give white opaque glazes, which contrast well with the smoked black or gray body. Mix oxides and stains into glazes for a variety of colors, some of which have a metallic sheen: 2–3 percent copper produces a turquoise that turns copper red when heavily reduced; and combinations of nickel and iron can create a silvery film. Raku glazes craze, and a network of black lines and spots is characteristic of this kind of firing. Apply your glazes thickly to achieve the best results, and make sure the glazed pots are perfectly dry before firing. Any damp areas flake away on meeting the heat inside the kiln.

Right: David Jones, Raku fired bowls

Can I pack my pots for a bisque firing so that they are touching?

Make full use of space

Pots made of undecorated clay, or those with a slip coating, can be packed tightly for a bisque firing. Pots can touch and be set inside each other to make maximum use of the space. Be sure to pack the pots so that they are supported by the bases and footrings of the pots beneath them (below left). Do not allow the rims to carry the weight of other pots (below right), which will lead to cracking and warping. Be aware that decoration including oxides may transfer to clay that touches it, and arrange your pots to prevent this from happening.

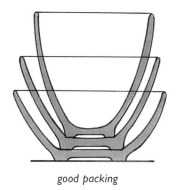

good packing

bad packing

Should I use the same firing cycle for a bisque firing and a glaze firing?

When clay is fired for the first time, as in a bisque firing, it must undergo a slow rise in temperature while water is given off and chemical changes take place. Potters therefore usually start their kilns slowly, moving from 25 percent power to 50 percent power in the first few hours. When the kiln is at 930–1110°F (500–600°C), bungs are put in place, and the kiln is switched to full power.

Pots that have already undergone heat changes, such as those that have been bisque fired, do not need to be heated so slowly during the initial stages of firing. Glaze firings, therefore, usually follow a different cycle from bisque firings. In the later stages of a glaze firing many potters slow the kiln, or soak it at top temperature, in order to mature the glaze fully. When completing pots in one firing instead of two – in the case of raw glazed ware, for example – you must consider both of these firing cycles, and perhaps combine a slow temperature rise at the start of the firing with a soak at top temperature.

I have a top-loading kiln. How can I judge where to place each succeeding shelf?

Checking the height clearance

When all the pots of one layer are packed, and you have built up the kiln props to what looks like a suitable height, place a flat stick across the top of the props. You will soon see if any of your pots are taller than the props, and if more clearance is needed before the next shelf can be set in place. Another way of assessing the necessary height of shelves is to build a set of props alongside your tallest pots. Do this on a table or shelf where you can view the work from the side, and establish an accurate measure.

Some of my tallest pots broke in the bisque firing. What could have happened?

When clay is fired it expands a little before shrinking. If you pack the kiln with a shelf too close to the top of the pots, the clay has nowhere to go when it expands, and is likely to crack or warp. Allow more space between the top of your pots and the next shelf to solve this problem.

What are the important things to remember when I pack a glaze firing?

Glaze melts and sticks to anything it touches. Be sure, therefore, that wherever a pot touches a shelf, you wipe it clean of glaze. Leave a space between pots so that they do not stick together. The heat at stoneware temperatures puts a heavy strain on kiln furniture. Check your props and shelves regularly for cracks and damage, and place shelves securely on props to avoid any danger of collapse. Pack the kiln in a balanced way, so that the heat can move through all areas of the kiln evenly.

How do I apply battwash to my shelves to make a smooth coating?

Use a thin mixture
Although you need a thick coating of battwash on your shelves, do not apply this in one layer. The shelves soak up liquid so quickly that a thick mixture of battwash forms into lumps.

1. Make up a thin mixture of battwash and water to the consistency of milk, and paint it on your shelves in several layers, using a wide, household paintbrush.

2. Check the edges of your shelves and remove any excess battwash with a damp sponge. If you allow this to remain, it may chip away as you pack the kiln, and fall onto pots below.

My new kiln shelves are becoming damaged with bits of glaze and vitrified clay. What can I do to protect them during firing?

Create a protective layer
Before using new shelves in your kiln, you should coat them with a layer of battwash or alumina hydrate. This helps to protect them from drops of glaze, oxide particles, and chips of vitrified clay that stick less readily to this surface than to the raw shelves. Clean and re-coat the shelves at regular intervals to maintain an even surface for your pots to stand on. You can also use a fine layer of silica sand. As you pack the kiln, smooth silica sand all over the shelf, and place your pots on this. When you unpack the kiln, remove the sand as you empty each shelf. The disadvantage of this method is that unless you are extremely careful, you can end up with sand all over the kiln, and in work that is about to be fired as well as underneath it.

Support the work
When you know that your glazes are very fluid and may run onto the shelves, place your work on kiln sitters. These are small disks of unglazed clay, which you can buy or make yourself. The sitters may be ruined with flowing glaze, but they are easy to remove from pots and far cheaper to replace than kiln shelves. Support fully glazed earthenware pots on trivets, to raise them from the kiln shelves. Although they stick in the glaze, the sharp tips of the trivets can be broken off to release the pot, and any damaged areas sanded over. Choose a trivet that will support your pot completely or the clay will warp out of shape during the firing.

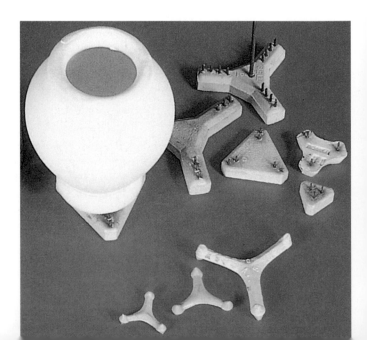

My pots are rough underneath and scratch the furniture, even though I smooth them with a sponge during making. What else can I do to resolve this?

Carborundum stones

Smoothing your pots with a sponge when the clay is wet can bring sand and grog to the surface. You need to grind rough bases after the clay has been fully fired. In the case of high-fired stoneware, this requires an extremely tough material. Carborundum stones, which are used to sharpen tools and sand metal objects, work efficiently on even the hardest ceramic. They can be purchased from hardware and art supply stores.

Clay grinding bars

You can rub two pots together, so that the bases sand each other, provided both are made of the same clay. There is, however, a risk of chipping one of the pots. It is better to make your own grinding bars.

1. Wedge sand or grog into a small lump of clay, so that it acquires a coarse texture. Make several such balls, with varying amounts of coarse material, to provide a range of textures.

2. Roll out the balls, and cut each resulting slab into thick bars. Rub over the bars with a damp sponge to raise the coarse material to the surface. Dry the bars and fire them in a glaze firing, so that they reach the highest temperature to which your pots are subjected.

3. Use your selection of grinding bars to rub the bases of your fired pots and remove rough surfaces.

My kiln turned itself off at temperature, but my glazes are still underfired. Why is this, and how do I make sure the glaze fires properly?

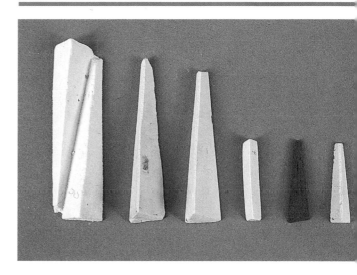

Use cones

Although we say that a glaze fires to a certain temperature, it is actually the heatwork that affects the melt of the glaze. A kiln that fires to a given temperature in 10 hours has undergone more heatwork than a kiln that has fired to the same temperature in only 7 hours, for example. You will get a more accurate reading of what is happening in the kiln by using cones. These are made from the same materials as glazes and melt according to the heatwork. They can also be affected by the rate of temperature rise and so it is important to use the same firing cycle when possible.

Use a wide firing glaze

There are glazes that are very temperamental and are ruined by a small rise or fall of the top temperature. Others produce good results over a wide range of temperatures, and these glazes are certainly more useful. If you do not want to worry about firing your kiln to exact temperatures and reproducing firing cycles with uniform heatwork, use a wide firing glaze that will give you consistent results.

I had to turn my kiln off before it reached temperature, but the glaze had overfired. How is this possible?

When an element burns out during firing, the kiln may continue to fire without reaching the top temperature or may take much longer than usual to do so. The heatwork is therefore greater than when all the components are functioning properly, and that is why your glazes were overfired. It is useful to put cones in the kiln where you can see them during firing. You can then turn the kiln off when the correct amount of heatwork has occurred, even if the designated temperature has not been reached. Some controllers allow you to set a time limit as well as a temperature limit. These are preferable if you cannot return to the kiln for days at a time.

How do I stand a cone securely?

Use a cone support or a coil of clay

A cone stand, which you can buy from your ceramic supplier, holds cones in the correct position during firing. This is particularly useful when more than one cone is used. However, the simplest way to secure cones is to wrap a coil of clay around the base.

1. You must start with the cone standing in the correct position. Stand the cone on a table or shelf, so that the base of the cone is fully in contact with the flat surface. The cone does not stand completely upright but is slanting. This is its correct position.

2. Roll a small coil of clay, and wrap it snugly around the base of the cone. Hold the cone on the table as you do this, to maintain its correct slanting position. A narrow wall is sufficient to support the cone, so remove any excess. Your cone is now ready to go into the kiln.

Should I use more than one cone, and if so, how should I position them?

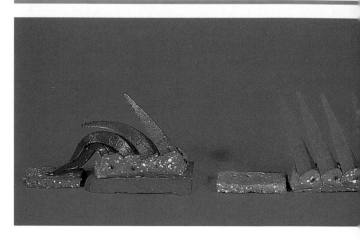

Positioning your cones

It is useful to place three cones in the kiln for each firing: a cone that melts just below the temperature you require; a cone that melts at the temperature you require; and a cone that melts just above the temperature you require. That way, you will have an early warning that your kiln is about to reach the firing temperature you want; an indication that the temperature has been achieved and you must switch the kiln off; and evidence to show if the kiln has overfired. You must position the cones in such a way that they do not melt onto one another. Stand them in a slanting line, beginning with the cone that will melt first.

Should I switch off the kiln when the cones start to bend, or when they are fully melted?

Consistency is the watchword here. Your kiln should be switched off at the same point every time to ensure that the same amount of heatwork has occurred. Many potters choose the point when the cone is bending enough to touch the kiln shelf as the indication for switching off the kiln. This is an easier stage to judge accurately than when a cone is bending in the air. You can take a different point of reference, however, if you feel it gives you better results, provided you can judge that point in the firing precisely and consistently.

When the door of my front-loading kiln is shut, it is too dark to see my cones. How can I tell that I have positioned them correctly?

To check that the cones are correctly positioned in front of the spy hole, create a light source around them as you put them in place. A candle, small flashlight, or even a lighted match will help you to complete this job successfully.

When I look into the firing kiln to read the cones, I cannot see them through the bright glare. How can I view them more easily?

Use a protective viewer

Looking through a spy hole when the kiln has reached a high temperature can damage your eyes, and the glare from the kiln usually makes it impossible to view the cones. View the cones through a piece of green glass, a special cone viewer, or, best of all, protective goggles. Shine a flashlight into the glare as you look through the goggles and the cones will stand out as dark shadows.

Why can't I keep the bungs in the kiln at the beginning of a firing, to get a quicker rise in temperature?

As the clay begins to heat up, water is given off as steam. If this is not allowed to escape through the bung holes, it can damage the interior of the kiln, the elements, and your work. Later in the firing cycle, gases and impurities burn away. Trapping these inside a sealed kiln can reduce the supply of oxygen and cause problems of bloating or dunting clay.

When should I put the bungs in the kiln, and when can I take them out again?

Putting bungs in

A temperature of 1110°F (600°C) is required to make sure that all the steam and many of the impurities have escaped from the clay. It is then safe to put the bungs in and seal the kiln. Many potters use the slightly lower temperature of 930°F (500°C). Your controller will indicate when your kiln has reached this temperature. A bright red glow will be visible through the bung holes.

Removing bungs

Removing the bungs when the kiln is at top temperature is not usually recommended, because it causes a drastic reduction in temperature that can split or craze the clay and glazes. Fired clay undergoes a chemical change at about 435°F (225°C). Leave the bungs in your kiln until it has cooled to below 390°F (200°C) to be sure that drafts of cold air will not damage the work. Some special firing sequences, such as those for crystal glazes, call for immediate cooling when the kiln reaches the top temperature but this is exceptional.

I can hear pinging noises coming from my kiln. What is causing them?

The chemical change that occurs when fired clay cools to about 435°F (225°C) results in sudden shrinkage. If you open the kiln too soon, while the pots are hotter than this crucial temperature, drafts of cold air can cause the clay and glazes to contract violently. This is what is making the pinging noise. Even if the temperature of the kiln reads below 390°F (200°C), there can be a buildup of heat in the kiln furniture and clay work, and it is better to delay opening your kiln until it is cool enough to touch.

Many of my pots have warped in the firing. How can I prevent this?

Handle pots carefully
Clays sometimes have a "memory." Pots that have been knocked out of shape and then repaired can return to their misshapen form during a high firing. Porcelain and smooth stoneware clays are particularly prone to this phenomenon. Take great care when handling items such as thrown bowls not to damage the shape. You can reduce the risk by wedging some molochite, grog, or sand into the clay to create a body that is less prone to such warping, but this will inevitably alter the texture of your finished work.

Packing the kiln
As you pack your kiln, leave a gap of at least 2in (5cm) between the pots and the elements, so that direct heat does not pull the clay out of shape. This is especially important with tall pots, which warp toward the heat if the elements are too close. Pack bowls

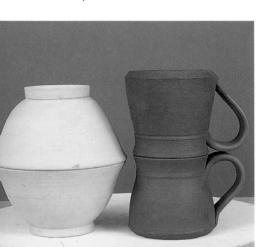

and mugs with the same-sized rims together for a bisque firing to help them stay perfectly round. You can do this for a glaze firing also but only if their rims are unglazed.

My flatware cracked during firing. What did I do wrong?

Place in sand
Cracking can occur because your flatware sticks to the shelf. To prevent this, dust your shelves with a fine layer of silica sand or alumina hydrate, and place your work on top. The bases can then move more easily as they shrink.

Cool the kiln before opening
Although the controller may show that the kiln temperature is below 390°F (200°C), kiln shelves retain the heat longer than the surrounding air. Flatware that is lying against the hot shelves will also stay hot, and letting cold air into the kiln may cause splitting or dunting as the clay contracts. Leave your kiln to cool completely before opening.

Sometimes my clay fires with unsightly little blisters. What can I do to prevent this?

First, consider whether you are overfiring your clay. Check with your clay supplier the maximum temperature for your clay and make sure that you are not exceeding it. Some clays are prone to bloating at high temperatures if carbon and other impurities have not escaped during firing. It is the bisque cycle and not the glaze firing that usually needs altering. Slow your bisque firing, particularly as you reach 1650–1830°F (900–1000°C). Take the bisque firing several degrees higher, or soak for half an hour at top temperature. These changes should allow unwanted gases to burn off more efficiently. You can also try packing the kiln with more space between pots, so that air can circulate better.

Some of my pots are always spoiled in the firing. Will I ever manage to make all of them right?

It is not possible to control everything that happens in the firing of your work. This is something that potters learn to live with, and even the most experienced lose a percentage of their work. You can reduce your loss rate if you make all your pots with care, give attention to every process they undergo, and study any disasters to learn from your mistakes. As you gain experience of your materials, and of making and firing techniques, you will have a better understanding of the extent to which each process can be controlled. But always remember that the unpredictable nature of firing clay can be one of the exciting aspects of pottery.

The handles on my mugs have pulled out of shape. What should I do?

Examine your pots

Handles can warp because of problems in the making of the pot. The area to which the handle is attached may be too thin to support the handle, or the handle may be excessively heavy. Your clay can aggravate the problem if it is very plastic. Mix in some grog or sand to make a coarser, stronger body, or switch to a clay with a greater resistance to warping.

Pack the kiln correctly

Handles need to be protected in the kiln. If they are placed close to the elements, they will be drawn toward the heat and will warp the pot to which they are attached. Pack the pots with their handles pointing inward, so that each handle is protected from the heat by the body of a pot.

I wipe the glaze off my jars and lids, but they stick together when fired. Should I fire them separately?

Fire lids in place

It is always a risk to fire pots and lids separately, because the smallest variation in the shape of either can prevent them from fitting together after firing. If you fire the lids on the pots, there is a much better chance that any slight warping will affect both. In fact, the presence of the lid often helps to support the rim and retain the shape of the pot. There are several methods of creating a barrier between the pot and lid to prevent them from sticking.

USE A WAX RESIST

Before you glaze your pots and lids, paint them with a special wax resist mixture which keeps the two pieces from adhering during the firing. Add a little battwash to some liquid wax, and paint the wax mixture onto the rims of your pots and lids. Set the pots and lids aside until the wax is completely dry. Glaze the pots and lids inside and out.

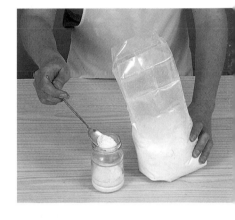

Although the waxed areas resist glaze, it is necessary to wipe them over with a wet sponge to remove the glaze completely. Put all the lids onto their pots for firing. Any residue left by the battwash after firing is easily cleaned away with sandpaper.

COAT RIMS AFTER GLAZING

After glazing, wipe the rim areas of your pots and lids as usual. Then apply a solution of china clay and alumina hydrate. This will enable you to fire the lids in place without their sticking. Alternatively, form some small balls of china clay and place them around the rims of the pots. Squash the balls as you push the lids into place. Residue from both the alumina hydrate mixture and the china clay balls can be sanded away after firing.

What is the difference between a reduction and an oxidized firing?

A change in atmosphere

In an oxidized firing, there is enough oxygen in the atmosphere to combine with the metals in the clay and glaze. Carbon dioxide gas is given off. This type of firing is produced in an electric kiln. In a reduction firing, the oxygen in the kiln is restricted. Oxygen is drawn from the metals that are present in the clay and glaze, causing color changes. Reduction firings use combustible fuels and carbon monoxide is given off, so this type of kiln requires an extraction system. The tile on the left was given an oxidized firing; the tile on the right a reduction firing.

How can I tell if my kiln is reducing?

Open the bung at the front of your kiln. If your kiln is reducing, a flame will burn out of the hole. Another indication is flames licking around the base of the flue or firebox. You can only learn to judge the degree of reduction in your particular kiln and its effects on your work by firing the kiln several times. There is an instrument that will record the amount of oxygen in the kiln and the type of atmosphere present, but it is costly.

How can I keep the temperature rising in a reduction firing?

Many kilns do not show a rise in temperature while reducing. A very careful setting of the reduction flame is usually needed, and if the reduction is too heavy, the temperature will fall. You can change to a firing cycle that includes phases of oxidized firing when the temperature rises between periods of reduction. If the temperature does not rise when the kiln is oxidizing, you need to increase the fuel to reach the required temperature.

Can I create a reduction atmosphere in my electric kiln?

Introducing reducing material

A reduction atmosphere can be created in an electric kiln by introducing materials that smolder, and burn up the oxygen present. These include mothballs, pine needles, grass and leaves, oil-soaked rags, or a gas poker. The reduction is usually done after the kiln has reached top temperature and has cooled down to about 1830°F (1000°C). The material is then introduced through a bung hole or by opening the kiln slightly. Luster glazes are an example of the effects that can be achieved in this way.

There are some major drawbacks in using an electric kiln for reduction firing. Electric kilns are not usually equipped with the extraction systems necessary to remove the emissions produced. Elements become damaged and will need replacing frequently. Having an oxidized firing between reduction firings will help to counteract this.

Above: Pauline Monkcom, Luster-glazed pitcher

Local reduction glazes

You can create the characteristic color responses of reduced glazes by mixing certain materials with your usual glaze ingredients to create a localized reduction. A glaze containing copper will thus turn red, and one using iron will turn green. Typical additions are silicon carbide, charcoal, sawdust, and carbon.

How do I keep the lovely burnished sheen on my pots? It seems to disappear when they are fired.

Many clays lose the sheen created by burnishing above a temperature of 1740–1830°F (950–1000°C). Keep to a low-temperature firing if you wish to retain this surface quality. No matter how high you fire your burnished pots, however, the smoothness of the surface will remain, and you can restore the shine with wax. Heat your pot slightly and rub wax into the surface, letting it melt into the clay. Allow the pot to cool, and rub it over with a rag or brush to create a polished shine. Wood wax, shoe polish, and marble wax work well. The clear polishes tend to enhance the color of the clay, whereas the colored varieties deepen tonal values.

What is the best way to fire my kiln when using prepared liquid lusters?

An enamel or luster firing can be a fast firing, taking only a few hours to reach 1380–1560°F (750–850°C). It is advisable to give the pots an initial slow heating for the first half-hour, so that thermal shock does not shatter them, after which you can switch the kiln to full. Leave all the bungs open throughout the firing, so that gases can escape and not cloud the lusters. The fumes given off during a luster firing are toxic. The kiln must be well ventilated and fired away from people.

What can I use as a chamber in which to smoke-fire pots?

Making firing chambers

Pots can be smoke-fired in any container that will withstand the heat.

I. Possible choices include metal garbage cans and buckets, chambers made of bricks, or a pit in the ground. Surround pots with sawdust, and use a top layer of newspaper to help light the sawdust.

2. Any chamber must have a suitable covering, because if too much air reaches the material, it will burn too fiercely and not produce the smoldering effect required. A kiln shelf or metal tray often provides an adequate lid.

Use your kiln
You can smoke pots in your kiln by placing them in a sagger, which you can buy or make yourself. This is a rectangular or cylindrical lidded box, built from a heavily sanded or grogged clay. Put your pots in the sagger on a layer of sawdust or woodchippings, and pack more of this material all around them. Place the sagger in the kiln with the lid fitted and fire the kiln in the usual way up to 1830°F (1000°C). The combustible material will smoke inside the sagger as the kiln is firing.

You can achieve a simple form of smoking in your kiln by using cooking foil. Wrap your pot in strips of newspaper and cover with foil. Leave a cavity of air inside the foil to allow the smoke to circulate. Seal the foil parcel, place in your kiln, and fire to a temperature of up to 1830°F (1000°C).

 *What sort of pots can I smoke?*

Smoke pots at different stages

It is possible to smoke pots at all stages – from unfired, dry clay, through bisque-fired pots, to glazed pieces – but the results will be different. Unfired clay pots are very porous, and because they absorb a lot of carbon, they can often be a dense black after a smoked firing. You must expect high losses with these pots, and those that remain will be soft, due to the low temperatures attained. Smoking glazed pots can create subtle variegation in the glaze, but again, some will crack due to thermal shock. Bisque-fired pots are excellent for smoking, because they have strength from their first firing but are sufficiently porous to produce dramatic effects.

Left: Peter Cosentino, Sections – sawdust smoked after glazing

Below: Jane Perryman, Coiled, smoke-fired vase

What materials should I burn in a smoked firing?

Combustible materials

The most widely used materials for smoked firings are wood products, such as sawdust and woodchippings. You can obtain these from numerous sources, such as carpentry and hardware stores, and lumber suppliers. The finer material produces a slower firing and denser color. Avoid sawdust from composition boards, which contains a great deal of glue and is a health hazard. Experiment with other materials, such as leaves, paper, and straw, combined with sawdust or used on their own, to produce variegated patterns from your smoking.

I would like the color of my smoked pots to be a light gray instead of dark black. How can I alter the color?

Control the density of smoke

One method is to lessen the density of the smoke. Fill your chamber with material but pack it very loosely. Coarse woodchippings, twigs, or paper burn quickly and yield a lighter smoking than fine sawdust.

Use a high bisque firing

Another method is to fire your pots to a higher temperature during a bisque firing so that they will be less porous. The effect of the smoke will then be reduced, resulting in a lighter color. A bisque firing of about 2010°F (1100°C) will produce a lighter gray than a firing of 1650°F (900°C), as demonstrated here. You can also smoke fully fired glazed pots for very subtle smoked effects.

How do I finish my pots after a smoked firing?

Enhance the surface of smoked pots

When you remove your pots from a smoked firing, they are covered in ash and even after cleaning they usually look dull. Additional treatment is needed for the true subtlety of the smoked markings to appear.

1. Wash your pots in water to remove ash, resists, and any tar left by the smoking material. You may need to scrub quite hard with an abrasive cloth, such as those used for cleaning saucepans, to dislodge some of this debris.

2. When your pots are dry, heat them, and rub wax over the surface so that it melts into the clay. Let the pots cool, and polish them with a rag or brush to enhance the tactile quality and color of the clay.

How can I encourage the smoke to create interesting patterns on my pots?

Use resists

Create patterns by applying resists to your pots before they are smoked. Slip, coils of clay, wire, tapes, and string can all be used to produce attractive effects.

1. Mix a slip that contains coarse material, such as sand, grog, or paper pulp, which helps it to remain in place on the pot. Paint patterns or block out areas of your pot.

2. Assemble a range of experimental pots using other resists, such as a pot wrapped in wire and another in lacy material. Each type of resist produces its own particular markings.

3. The smoke acts around the resists to form a subtle pattern rather than a clear-cut design. After the smoked firing, clean away the residue of the resists, and wax your pots. Possibilities for patterns are endless, and add greatly to the interest and beauty of smoke-fired pots.

Creating color

You can create flashes of color on your smoke-fired pots by introducing oxides in one of several ways. Mix copper and some salt into the sawdust around your pots; rub or spray parts of the pots with copper or iron; or wrap the pots in straw or rags soaked in copper and salt. A solution of copper or iron sulfate is better than oxides for this work, because it is much weaker and produces subtle color effects. Other methods of introducing color are to make your pots in colored clay or coat them in shades of colored slip before bisque firing.

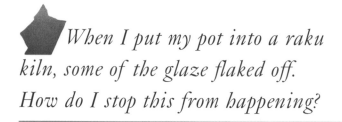

What equipment do I need for a raku firing?

Special equipment

A raku firing is exceptional in that the pots (usually bisqueware) are placed inside a kiln that has been heated above 1560°F (850°C), and once the temperature is high enough to melt the glaze, the pots are removed from the kiln.

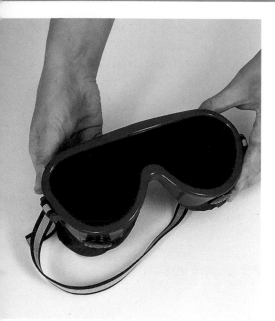

You need special equipment for raku firing that allows you to work with a red-hot kiln efficiently and safely. Raku kilns are generally fueled by gas or propane and can be of loose brick or fiber construction. They should have a fast temperature climb, and allow you to open the door and reach in to place or retrieve work easily. Some kilns are constructed so that the kiln body is moved to allow access to the work. Raku kilns are available from clay suppliers, or you can purchase separate items, such as a burner, fiber blanket, and metal container, to construct your own.

It is essential to have additional equipment to protect you from the heat. Raku tongs (left), which have long handles, a good pair of protective gauntlets, and goggles (above left) will enable you to maneuver hot work during the raku process. When the pots are removed, they are usually smothered in sawdust, leaves, or other combustible organic material to cause a reduction atmosphere. Sometimes they are quenched in water. You will need metal buckets or other suitable containers for these procedures.

When I put my pot into a raku kiln, some of the glaze flaked off. How do I stop this from happening?

The glaze must be absolutely dry before it meets the tremendous heat of the raku kiln. If not, chunks will peel away from the clay body of the pot. The best way to dry a glazed pot is to place it near or on top of the kiln as it is heating up. You can dry pots like this as they await their turn to go into the kiln.

The glaze on my raku pieces has not melted fully. How can I tell when the kiln has reached the proper temperature for the glaze?

Reading the kiln

When the correct firing temperature is achieved, the kiln will glow bright red, with no dull areas around your pots, and the glaze on your work will look shiny all over, indicating that the glaze is fully melted. These signs may not be obvious at first, but you will come to recognize them with experience.

Testing the temperature

You can read the temperature in the kiln using a pyrometer. This will not tell you the amount of heatwork that the glaze has endured, however. Use small rings or lumps of clay to help you assess the melt of the glaze. Bisque fire and glaze these test pieces in the same way as your work, and place them alongside your pots in the kiln. Remove a test piece at intervals throughout the firing, until you are sure that the glaze has melted correctly.

Is it possible to use my electric kiln for raku firings?

It is possible to use small electric kilns for raku firing, but there are some serious risks you must consider first. Raku firings usually necessitate covering the hot, fired pots in material that will enable the process of reduction to turn the clay body black. The resultant steam and smoke mean that this operation must be performed outside. A raku kiln must therefore be located within easy reach of the open air. This is not usually the case with electric kilns.

During raku firing you must be able to maneuver pots into and out of a red-hot kiln with ease. Touching a live element in an electric kiln with metal tongs could be fatal. You must switch the kiln off and unplug it every time you prepare to reach inside. You must also check with the kiln manufacturer whether there is any possibility of residual electricity remaining in an element after the kiln has been switched off. You can increase your safety by building a clay, brick, or fiber box to act as a firing chamber inside the kiln. Electric kilns are not manufactured to undergo the stresses of a raku firing, with its rapid and extreme changes in temperature. You risk damaging the elements and the brickwork of your kiln with continual raku firing.

I have heard that salt fuming is very toxic. Is there a less harmful alternative?

You can replace the salt with soda ash or sodium carbonate, which produces less toxic fumes. The glaze coating produced from these materials is not quite the same as that from salt. Adapt to the surface qualities that these materials offer rather than making a comparison with salt firing.

The cones in my salt firing did not melt properly. Why was this?

Cones placed in a salt kiln become covered in the glaze coating as well as everything else in the kiln. That is why they do not react in the normal way. A better method of reading the heatwork in the kiln is to use rings of clay. Place these in the kiln where you can easily remove them during the course of firing. The coating of glaze on the clay rings will indicate the thickness and quality of the glaze produced by the salting process and whether the firing is complete.

Will it harm my gas kiln if I experiment with salt firing?

Build a salt kiln

Salt will coat everything in the kiln, including the walls and furniture. You can protect these with a solution of china clay and alumina, but every subsequent firing will be affected by the residue left inside the kiln. Salt firing requires a salt kiln. Perhaps you could put a few experiments into the salt kiln of another potter, and build your own salt kiln if you decide to adopt this type of firing.

Above: Jane Hamlyn, Salt-glazed quatrefoil dish

Glossary

Agateware
Pottery made from clay of different colors that have been mixed to give a marbled effect. Named after the stone agate, which it resembles.

Bat
Used to describe different flat surfaces in the pottery workshop: a kiln bat is a kiln shelf; a plaster bat is a flat slab of plaster used for drying wet clay; a throwing bat is a removable disk placed on the wheelhead that allows a pot to be lifted easily, without distortion, immediately after throwing.

Bisqueware or Biscuitware
Pottery that has had a first firing, generally to 1830°F (1000°C), which has made the clay hard but still porous.

Body
The word that potters use to describe a particular mixture of clay. Some examples of clay bodies are: stoneware body, buff body, porcelain body.

Burnishing
Polishing the surface of leather-hard clay with a smooth tool to give the clay a smooth, shiny surface.

Ceramic
Clay that has been fired above 1110°F (600°C) so that it can no longer return to a plastic state.

Chuck
A hollow form made in clay or plaster which holds a pot securely during turning.

Collar
A thrown ring of clay that is usually added to an already thrown form so that the shape or height can be extended. For example, a collar can be added to a goblet cup in order to throw the stem, a bowl in order to throw a footring, or the body of a bottle in order to throw a tall neck.

Collaring
The action of squeezing around a pot in order to draw the shape inward. This technique is used particularly when pinching and throwing.

Cones
Small rods made from glaze materials that melt at set temperatures according to their number. They are affected by the heatwork of a firing kiln, and can therefore show what is happening to the glazes or clays in the same firing.

Firing/Firing Cycle
Heating clay in a kiln until it becomes hard and permanent. A firing cycle is the particular way in which the kiln is fired: the speed of temperature rise, the final top temperature, whether there are any periods of soak, the type of atmosphere used, and the rate of cooling.

Flux
An ingredient in a glaze or clay that causes it to melt readily, helping silica to form glaze or glass.

Footring
The circle of clay at the base of a pot that raises the form from the surface it is standing on.

Frit
A glaze material that has been fused with silica and finely ground to a powder. It is used as a less toxic ingredient in glazes, for example a lead frit in place of raw lead.

Greenware
Unfired pottery that is dry and waiting for a first firing.

Grog
Granules of pottery that have been fired and ground down. Grog is added to plastic clay to give texture or reduce shrinkage.

Kidney
A flat tool shaped like a kidney which can be made in wood, metal, rubber, or plastic. Kidneys are used to help shape and smooth the clay.

Leather-hard
The stage of drying when clay is no longer plastic, but is not dry and brittle. The clay resembles and handles rather like a piece of leather. This is the ideal stage for joining clay pieces together.

Plinth
A block or base made to rest a sculpture or decorative piece on.

Prop
A kiln prop is the tubular sections of kiln furniture on which the shelves rest. They are used to build up the height between layers in the kiln. A prop is also a support used when building or firing clay work.

Raku
A Japanese firing technique in which pots are placed directly into a hot kiln and removed when red-hot.

Slip
Clay which is in a liquid state. There are various types of slip. The term may refer to a mixture of clay and water that is used when joining clay pieces together; decorating slip which also has color added; or casting slip which is used in molds to produce pottery items.

SAFETY INFORMATION

* Keep your workshop clean to minimize the dust from clay or glaze materials. You will need a good mop and bucket, and a vacuum cleaner that can cope with wet as well as dry material. An air filter unit will improve the quality of the air in your workshop.
* Use covered containers or heavyweight plastic bags for storing your raw materials.
* Label all containers, and check out storage and safety requirements with the supplier.
* Make sure you have adequate ventilation and extraction for your kiln and spray equipment.
* Check all of the safety precautions necessary when installing and using your particular types of machinery. Be particularly vigilant when dealing with the heat and glare of a hot kiln. Only look into the firing kiln from a safe distance, and use a kiln viewer or safety goggles.
* Buy equipment such as bowls, buckets, spoons, sieves, and whisks that are kept for your pottery studio alone, and not shared with the domestic areas of your home.
* A dust mask is essential for your personal health. Keep it in a handy spot, so that you wear it whenever dust may be inhaled. Other personal equipment should include a washable apron, rubber gloves, and a towel and soap to clean your hands before leaving the studio. Keep a set of clothes for working in, and wash these regularly to minimize the build-up of clay dust in the material.

Index

Page numbers in *italics* refer to illustrations of artists' work.

Credits

The author and publisher would like to thank the following people for their help during the making of this book:

John Blackwell and **Cathy Littlejohn** for demonstrating some of the techniques featured in the photography;

Mike Bailey at Bath Potters Supplies for technical advice;

Graham Williamson for technical advice;

All of the potters who have kindly allowed us to reproduce examples of their work.

Quarto would also like to acknowledge and thank the following companies for supplying materials used in photography:

Bath Potters Supplies
2 Dorset Close
Bath
Avon BA2 3RF
Tel: (UK) 01225 337046
Fax: (UK) 01225 462712
Bath Potters supplied the vast majority of the materials and equipment used in photography.

Axner Pottery Supply
490 Kane Court
PO Box 621484
Oviedo FL 32762
Tel: (US) 407 365 2600
Fax: (US) 407 365 5573
Axner supplied the underglaze pens featured on page 134.

Cookson Matthey Ceramics & Materials Ltd
Uttoxeter Road
Meir
Stoke on Trent ST3 7XW
Tel: (UK) 01782 590000
Fax: (UK) 01782 590590
Cookson Matthey supplied the decals featured on page 152.

Left: Laszlo Fekete, Plastic